EAST SUSSEX

TOWN CENTRE MAPS

Street maps with index
Administrative Districts
Road Map with index
Postcodes

Scale of street plans: 4 In... ...ted)

≡ Motorway			∿	Stream / River
≡ 'A' Road / Dual			Lock ∿	Canal
≡ 'B' Road / Dual			→	One-way Street
≡ Minor Road / Dual			P	Car Park
≡ Track			C	Public Convenience
▨ Pedestrianized			i	Tourist Information
▬ Railway / Station			+	Place of Worship
- - - Footpath			●	Post Office

Every effo... the accur... ...this book but... ...publishers cannot accept responsibility for expense or loss caused by an error or omission. Information that will be of assistance to the user of the maps will be welcomed.

The representation on these maps of a road, track or path is no evidence of the existence of a right of way.

...eet plans prepared and published by ESTATE PUBLICATIONS, Bridewell House, TENTERDEN, KENT. The Publishers acknowledge the co-operation of the local authorities of towns represented in this atlas.

Ordnance Survey This product includes mapping data licensed from Ordnance Survey® with the permission of the Controller of Her Majesty's Stationery Office.

ISBN 1 84192 155 6

COUNTY RED BOOKS contain street maps for each town centre. The street atlases listed below are SUPER & LOCAL RED BOOKS, with comprehensive local covergae.

BRIGHTON

including: Hove, Lewes, Newhaven, Portslade-by-Sea, Seaford, Shoreham-by-Sea etc.

CHICHESTER & BOGNOR REGIS

including: Bosham, East Wittering, Fishbourne, Middleton on Sea, Pagham, Selsey, West Wittering etc.

CRAWLEY & MID SUSSEX

including: Ashurst Wood, Burgess Hill, East Grinstead, Gatwick, Hassocks, Haywards Heath, Horsham etc.

EASTBOURNE

including: Lewes, Hailsham, Bexhill, Seaford, Cooden, Polegate, Pevensey etc.

HASTINGS & BEXHILL

including: Rye, Battle, Winchelsea, Camber, Fairlight, St. Leonards etc.

WORTHING & LITTLEHAMPTON

including: Angmering, Arundel, Goring by Sea, Henfield, Pulborough, Rustington, Steyning, Storrington etc.

For a complete title listing please visit our website
www.estate-publications.co.uk

CONTENTS

...MINISTRATIVE DISTRICTS: pages 4-5

...EX TO ROAD MAP: pages 6-7

...JNTY ROAD MAP: pages 8-11

...WN CENTRE STREET MAPS:

...ston	page 12	Mayfield	35
...e	13	Newhaven	37
...ill	14-15	Newick	38
...opstone	48	Northiam	38
...ton (Enlarged Centre)	16-17	Peacehaven	39
...ed	31	Pevensey	40
...ber	34	Pevensey Bay	41
...wborough	18-19	Polegate	42
...hling	35	Portslade-by-Sea	43
...bourne	20-21	Ringmer	47
...light Cove	23	Robertsbridge	51
...est Row	22	Rottingdean	44
...sham	25	Rye	46
...tings	26-27	St Leonards	50
...thfield	28	Saltdean	45
...stmonceux	29	Seaford	49
...am	29	South Heighton	36
...ve	30	Ticehurst	51
...esham	31	Uckfield	52-53
...ves (inc. Enlarged Centre)	32-33	Wadhurst	54
...ver Horsebridge	24	Westfield	56
...resfield	34	Winchelsea	55

...DEX TO STREETS: page 56

Scale of street plans: 4 Inches to 1 Mile (unless otherwise stated)

COUNTY RED BOOKS

...his atlas is intended for those requiring street maps of the historical and commercial centres of towns within the ...ounty. Each locality is normally presented on one or two pages and although, with many small towns, this space ...is sufficient to portray the whole urban area, the maps of large towns and cities are for centres only and are not intended to be comprehensive. Such coverage is offered in the Super and Local Red Book (see Page 2).

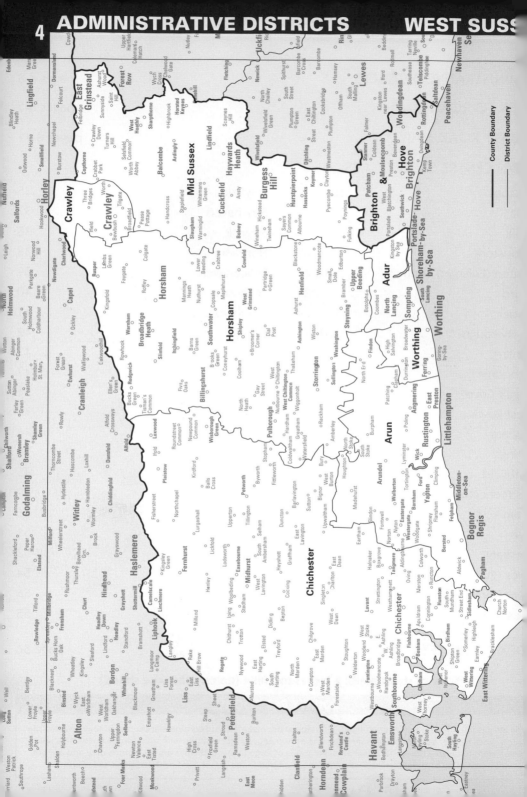

County Boundary
District Boundary

Kingsnorth · Shadoxhurst · Snargate · Brookland

Kenardington · Appledore · Stone

Betherden · Redbrook Street · Woodchurch · Reading Street · Iden · Camber

Haffenden Quarter · High Halden · St. Michaels · Leigh Green · Wittersham · Peasmarsh · Rye Harbour · East Guldeford

Standen · Biddenden · East End · Rolvenden · Small Hythe · Rye Foreign · Rye · Playden · Winchelsea Beach · Cliff End

Tenterden · Sissinghurst · Benenden · Rolvenden Layne · Newenden · Northiam · Four Oaks · Beckley · Udimore · Icklesham · Winchelsea

Fritterden · Cranbrook Common · Iden Green · Four Throws · Bodiam · Ewhurst Green · Staplecross · Cripp's Corner · Sedlescombe · Brede · Westfield · Fairlight

Brenchley · Curtisden Green · **Cranbrook** · Hartley · The Moor · **Hurst Green** · **Salehurst** · Vinehall Street · Catsfield · Crowhurst · Guestling Green · Ore · **Hastings**

Horsmonden · Goudhurst · **Hawkhurst** · **Robertsbridge** · Mill Corner · Broad Oak · Netherfield · **Battle** · **St. Leonards**

Matfield · Kilndown · Lamberhurst · Filmwell · Etchingham · Oxley's Green · **Rother** · Mountfield · Whatlington · **Sidley** · Bulverhythe

Royal · **Pembury** · Bells Yew Green · Three Leg Cross · **Ticehurst** · Stonegate · **Burwash** · Brightling · Penhurst · Hollington · **Bexhill**

Speldhurst · Langton Green · Frant · Tidebrook · Witherenden Hill · Burwash Common · Dallington · Ponts Green · Hooe · Little Common

Southborough · **Tunbridge Wells** · Eridge Green · Mark Cross · **Wadhurst** · Causeley Wood · Cade Street · Punnett's Town · Rushlake Green · Ninfield · Lunsford's Cross · Warting · **Pevensey Bay**

Fordcombe · Groombridge · Boarshead · **Mayfield** · Broad Oako · **Heathfield** · **Washbeach** · Foul Mile · Bodle Street Green · **Herstmonceux** · Windmill Hill · Pevensey · **Eastbourne**

Markbeech · Ashurst · Blackham · Eridge Green · **Rotherfield** · Five Ashes · Little London · **Horam** · Cowbeach · Magham Down · Hankham · Westham · **Langney**

Cowden · **Wightham** · Friar's Gate · Argos Hill · Cross in Hand · Vines Cross · **Hellingly** · Lower Horsebridge · **Hampden Park** · **Eastbourne**

East Grinstead · Felbridge · Fordcombe · Upper Hartfield · Coleman's Hatch · Hadlow Down · Waldron · **Wealden** · Chiddingly · Golden Cross · Upper Dicker · **Polegate** · Stone Cross · **Willingdon**

Newchapel · Felcourt · Saint Hill · **Forest Row** · Nutley · High Hurstwood · **Buxted** · Blackboys · **East Hoathly** · Whitesmith · Arlington · Folkington · Filching · Jevington · **Friston** · East Dean · Birling Gap

Dormansland · Ashurst Wood · Wych Cross · Chelwood Gate · Fairwarp · **Maresfield** · Halland · Laughton · Ripe · Chalvington · Wilmington · Litlington · Westdean

Burstow · Crawley Down · Turners Hill · Highbrook · **Uckfield** · Little Horsted · Shortgate · Glyndebourne · Selmeston · Alciston · Berwick · East Blatchington · **Seaford**

Copthorne · Selsfield Common · Sharpthorne · **Fletching** · **Newick** · Spithurst · Barcombe Cross · Glynde · Beddingham · Tarring Neville · **Newhaven**

East Grinstead · Sunnyside · **West Hoathly** · **Ardingly** · **Fletching** · Ridgewood · Isfield · Barcombe · Cooksbridge · South Malling · **Ringmer** · West Firle · Firle · Southease · Telscombe · Piddinghoe · **Peacehaven**

Turners Hill · Highbrook · **Horsted Keynes** · Scaynes Hill · North Chailey · South Street · **Lewes** · Offham · Hamsey · Iford · Rodmell · Denton

Crabbet Park · **Balcombe** · **Lindfield** · Wivelsfield Green · Ditchling · Westmeston · Kingston near Lewes · **Woodingdean** · **Saltdean**

Staplefield · Whiteman's Green · Staplefield · Wivelsfield · Plumpton · East Chiltington · Plumpton Green · **Rottingdean** · **Hove**

Worth Abbey · **Cuckfield** · **Hassocks** · Keymer · Clayton · Pyecombe · Falmer · Stanmer · **Patcham** · **Moulsecoomb** · Kemp Town

Slaugham · Warninglid · Ansty · **Burgess Hill** · **Hurstpierpoint** · Sayers Common · Albourne · Newtimber · **Brighton & Hove** · Preston · Bevendean · West Blatchington · **Brighton**

Pease Pottage · Bolney · Twineham · Hickstead · Poynings · Fulking · **Portslade-by-Sea** · **Hove** · Southwick

Handcross · Cowfold · Blackstone · **Hove** · **Portslade-by-Sea**

Hookwood · Charlwood · Lambs Green · Colgate · Crabtree · Cowfold · Edburton · Fulking · Kingston by Sea

Horley · **Crawley** · Three Bridges · Tilgate · Ifield · Broadfield · Worth

Hastings · **Eastbourne**

Hailsham

Crowborough

Haywards Heath

Alciston	9 D6	
Alfriston	9 E7	
Argos Hill	8 F3	
Arlington	9 E6	
Barcombe	9 C5	
Barcombe Cross	9 C5	
Battle	11 B5	
Beckley	10 D4	
Beddingham	9 D6	
Bells Yew Green	8 F2	
Berwick	9 E7	
Bevendean	9 B6	
Bexhill	11 B6	
Birling Gap	9 E8	
Bishopstone	9 D7	
Blackboys	8 E4	
Blackham	8 D1	
Boarshead	8 E2	
Bodiam	10 C3	
Bodle Street Green	11 A5	
Boreham Street	11 A6	
Brede	10 D4	
Brightling	10 A4	
Brighton	9 A7	
Broad Oak	8 F4	
Broad Oak	10 D4	
Bulverhythe	11 C6	
Burwash	10 B4	
Burwash Common	10 A4	
Buxted	8 E4	
Cade Street	8 F4	
Camber	10 F4	
Catsfield	11 B5	
Chalvington	9 E6	
Chelwood Gate	8 C3	
Chiddingly	9 E5	
Cliff End	11 E5	

Coldean	9 B6	
Coleman's Hatch	8 D2	
Cooksbridge	9 C5	
Cousley Wood	10 A2	
Cowbeech	9 F5	
Cripp's Corner	10 C4	
Cross in Hand	8 F4	
Crowborough	8 E3	
Crowhurst	11 B5	
Dallington	10 A4	
Danehill	8 C3	
Denton	9 D7	
Ditchling	9 B5	
East Blatchington	9 E7	
East Chiltington	9 C5	
East Dean	9 F8	
East Guldeford	10 F4	
East Hoathly	9 E5	
Eastbourne	11 A7	
Eridge Green	8 F2	
Etchingham	10 B3	
Ewhurst Green	10 C4	
Fairlight	11 D5	
Fairwarp	8 D3	
Falmer	9 B6	
Filching	9 F7	
Five Ashes	8 F3	
Fletching	8 C4	
Flimwell	10 B3	
Folkington	9 E7	
Forest Row	8 C2	
Foul Mile	11 A5	
Four Oaks	10 D4	
Framfield	8 E4	
Frant	8 F2	
Friar's Gate	8 E2	

Friston	
Glynde	
Glyndebourne	
Golden Cross	
Groombridge	
Guestling Green	
Hadlow Down	
Hailsham	
Halland	
Hampden Park	
Hamsey	
Hankham	
Hartfield	
Hastings	
Heathfield	
Hellingly	
Herstmonceux	
High Hurstwood	
Hollington	
Hooe	
Horam	
Hove	
Hurst Green	
Icklesham	
Iden	
Iford	
Isfield	
Jevington	
Kemp Town	
Kingston near Lewes	
Langney	
Laughton	
Lewes	

...ton	9 E7
...Common	11 B6
...Horsted	9 D5
...ondon	8 F4
...Horsebridge	9 F5
...rd's Cross	11 B6
...am Down	9 F6
...field	8 D4
...Cross	8 F3
...eld	8 F3
...orner	10 D4
...ecoomb	9 B6
...tfield	10 B4
...erfield	10 B4
...aven	9 C7
...ck	8 C4
...eld	11 B5
...Chailey	8 C4
...iam	10 D4
...y	8 D3
...m	9 C5
	11 D6
...gdean	9 B7
...'s Green	10 B4
...ham	9 A6
...ehaven	9 B7
...marsh	10 E4
...urst	11 B5
	11 E5
...nsey	11 A6
...nsey Bay	11 A7
...inghoe	9 C7
...den	10 E4
...pton	9 B5
...pton Green	9 B5
Polegate	9 E6
Ponts Green	11 A5
Portslade-by-Sea	9 A7
Poundgate	8 D3
Preston	9 B6
Punnett's Town	10 A4
Ridgewood	8 D4
Ringmer	9 D5
Ripe	9 E6
Robertsbridge	10 B4
Rodmell	9 C6
Rotherfield	8 F3
Rottingdean	9 B7
Rushlake Green	11 A5
Rye	10 E4
Rye Foreign	10 E4
Rye Harbour	10 F4
Saint Leonards	11 C6
Salehurst	10 C4
Saltdean	9 C7
Seaford	9 D7
Sedlescombe	11 C5
Selmeston	9 E6
Shortgate	9 D5
Sidley	11 B6
South Heighton	9 D7
South Malling	9 C5
South Street	9 C5
Southease	9 C7
Spithurst	9 C5
Stanmer	9 B6
Staplecross	10 C4
Stone Cross	9 F7
Stonegate	10 A3
Streat	9 B5
Tarring Neville	9 D7
Telscombe	9 C7
Three Leg Cross	10 A2
Ticehurst	10 A3
Tidebrook	8 F3
Uckfield	8 D4
Udimore	10 E4
Upper Dicker	9 E6
Upper Hartfield	8 D2
Vinehall Street	10 C4
Vines Cross	9 F5
Wadhurst	10 A3
Waldron	8 E4
Warbleton	8 F4
Wartling	11 A6
West Blatchington	9 A6
West Firle	9 D6
Westdean	9 E7
Westfield	11 D5
Westham	11 A7
Westmeston	9 B5
Whatlington	10 B4
Whitesmith	9 E5
Willingdon	9 F7
Wilmington	9 E7
Winchelsea	11 E5
Winchelsea Beach	11 E5
Windmill Hill	11 A6
Witherenden Hill	10 A3
Withyham	8 D2
Wivelsfield	8 B4
Wivelsfield Green	8 B4
Woodingdean	9 B6
Wych Cross	8 C3

Beach

Cliff End

Pett

Fairlight

Westfield

Guestling Green

Ore

A259

B2093

Hastings

Hollington

A2100

B2092

St. Leonards

Bulverhythe

Battle

Crowhurst

Catsfield

B2204

Lunsford's Cross

Ninfield

Hooe

Little Common

Sidley

Bexhill

A269

A271

B2095

Fouls Green

Bodle Street Green

Herstmonceux

Windmill Hill

Magham Down

Boreham Street

Wartling

Waller's Haven

A259

Pevensey Bay

Pevensey Bay

Langney Point

Pevensey

Westham

Langney

Eastbourne

Foul Mile

A271

A2280

Stone Cross

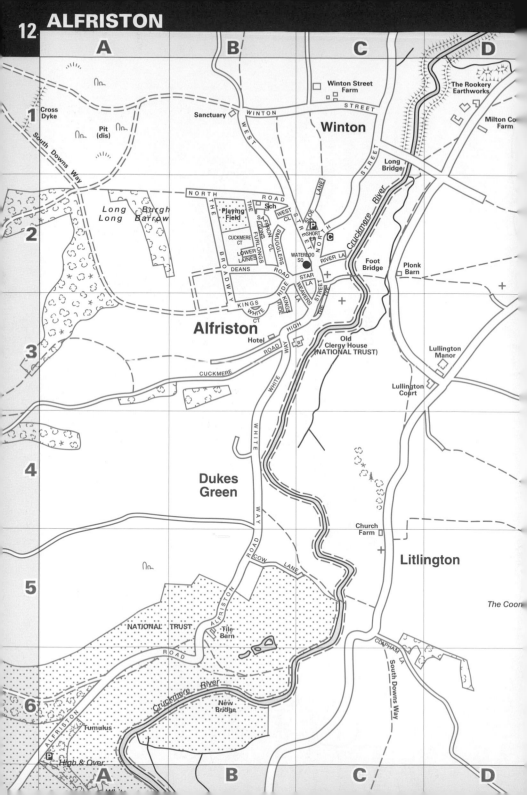

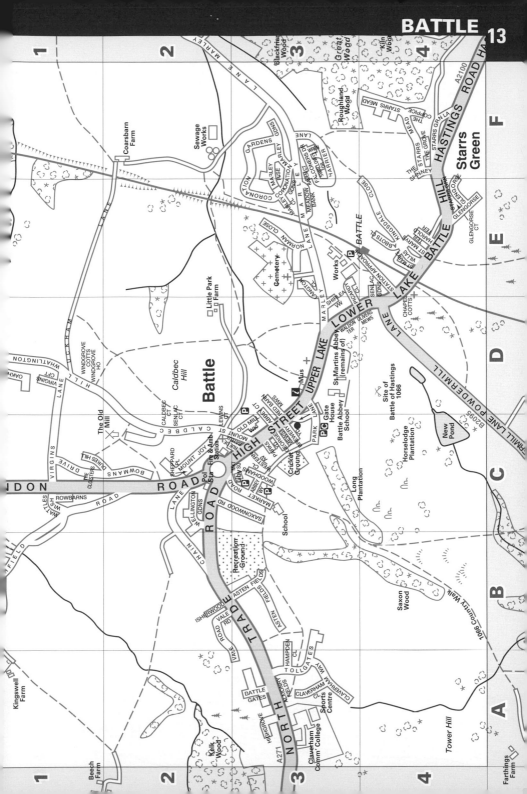

E F G H

Combe Wood

WORSHAM LANE

WORSHAM LANE

Pebsham Wood

Upper Worsham Farm

Pebsham Farm

FILSHAM LANE

PEBSHAM LANE

AMANDA
IAN CLOSE
GWYNETH
LESLEY
ANGELA
ALLEN
GROVE
CHRISTINE
BUCKHOLT AV
TOP CROSS RD
PEBSHAM DRIVE
DIANA

STWOOD

CHERRY TREE GDNS
CARDINALS
WILKINS WY
BISHOPS WALK
PENHURST DR
SILVA CL
GAVIN
ASTOR CL
LONG

PEBSHAM LANE

ROAD HASTINGS

ALFORD WAY
ROUNDACRES WY
PEBSHAM LA
MILLAND
GAMER
PEBSHAM GDNS
SEABOURNE GDNS
LABURNUM
ROWAN
MAYTREE GDNS
HASLAM
CRES
ROAD
SEABOURNE
CRES
MISTLEY CL

Pebsham

WANNOCK
THAKEN
-HAM CL
LULLING
-TON CL
MARTYNS
BARN CL
GLYNE
KINVER CL
DALLING-
TON CL
HURST
WOOD

Sch
CHARTRES CL
THE GLADES
C
CHARTRES CL
THE BRIARY
PORTERS
CONSTABLE WY
GEORG
JIAN
BEVIN
SANDOWN WY
BOORMAN
CL
TURNER RD
LANSDOWNE
GDNS
HASTINGS
ROAD
MAYFIELD
School
Sch
ROYSTON GDNS
THIRD AVENUE
SECOND AVENUE
GRAND AV
GLYNE DRIVE
CLAXTON CL
FAIRLIGHT
WAY
RD

HURST GDNS
THE THE
CROXFORD WY
WAY
ELMSTEAD RD
DORSET
PENLAND ROAD
School
Playing Field
FIRST AVENUE
WENTWORTH CL
ASCENT
GLYNE
GIBB CLOSE
GLYNE DRIVE
GLOUCESTER AV
YORK
KENT CL
LEWIS AV

Glyne Gap

BEXLEIGH AV
HYTHE AV
ABBEY DRIVE
BEXLEIGH AV

OFFA WAY

TORY
WARR
PETERS CT
HASTINGS RD
FAIRMOUNT RD

DE LA WARR ROAD

TIVERTON DR
CALLANS
CLIFTON RISE
GLASSENBURY RD
ROOKHURST RD
PENN LA
School
SCHOOL PLACE
BEAULIEU DR

BEXHILL ROAD

BE

A259

DORSET RD

MANOR RD
OLD MANOR CL
CHELSEA
MARTLETS COLLEGE
DE LA WARR
COLLEGE ROAD
COMPTON
EARL
KESTREL CL
SAXON RISE
KENNEDY RD
LINKS DRIVE
WINDHAM WY
VENTUOR CT
RIDGEWOOD
COLLEGE ROAD
BRIDGEWOOD
WINDHAM GARDENS
BRETT DRIVE
SNRD
BOXGROVE
IND EST

RAVENSIDE RETAIL & LEISURE PARK

EN RD
ASHDOWN
LINKS
DRIVE
THE FINCHES
Playing Field
School
GALLEY HILL VIEW
PLACE

Galley Hill

Pol Sta
Court
Nursing Home
CANTELUPE ROAD
DORSET RD
LIONEL RD
BROOK RD
BUCKHURST
SUTTON
PARADE
P

DE LA WARR PARADE
BEDFORD AV
BOLEBROOK RD
SSEX RD
C C

My Lords Rock

Lane End Rock

E F G H

1

2

3

4

5

6

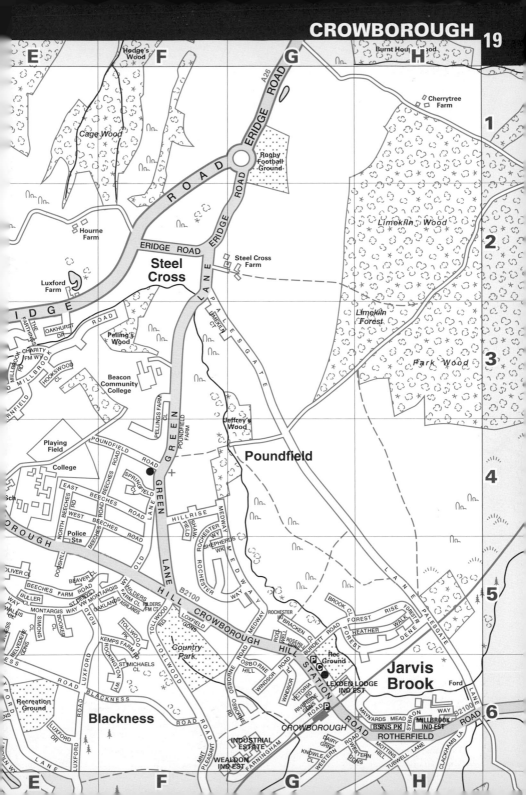

EASTBOURNE

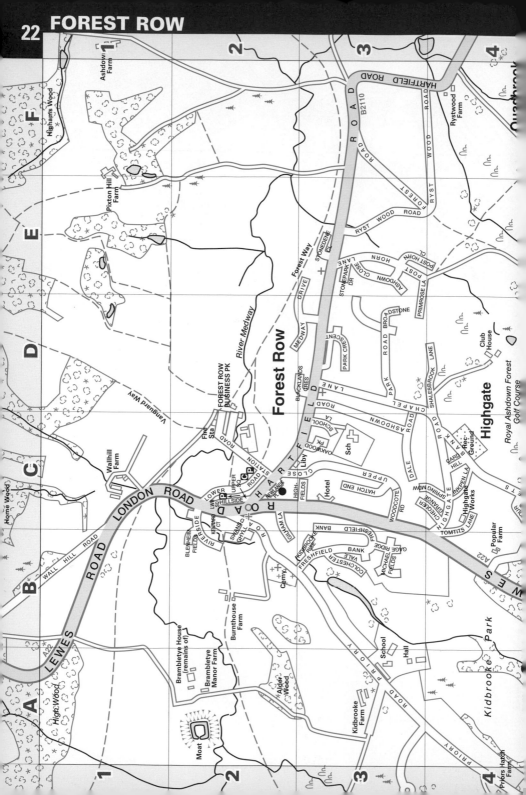

Hastings

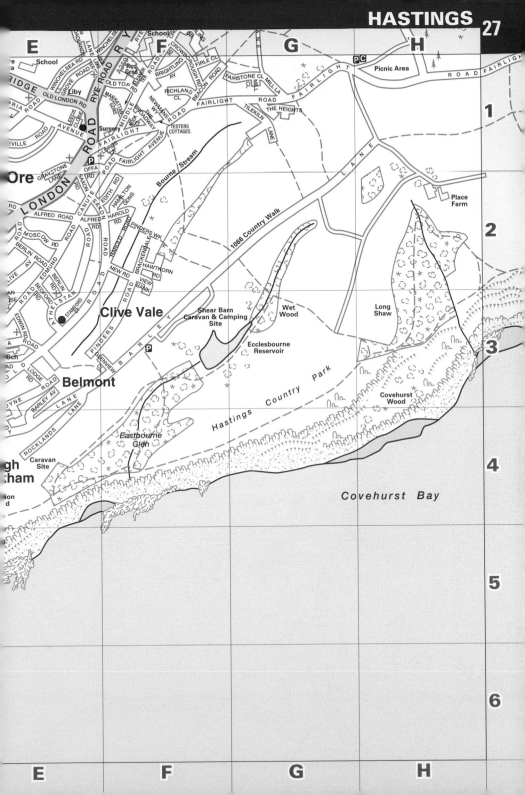

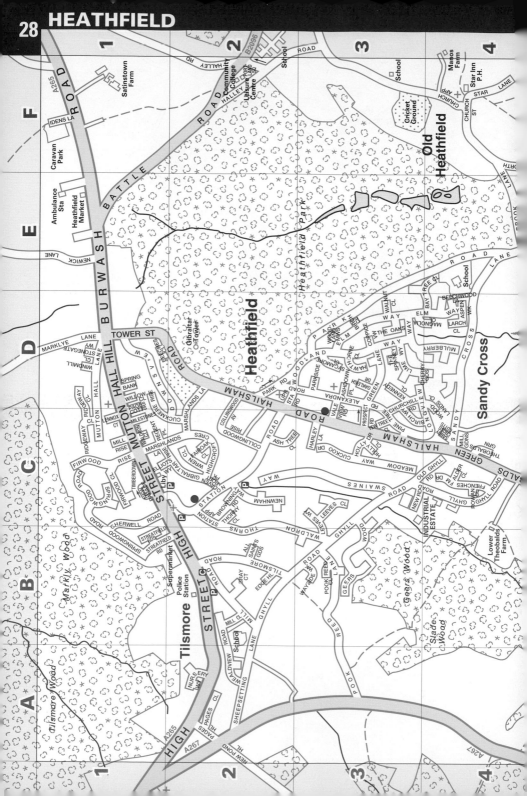

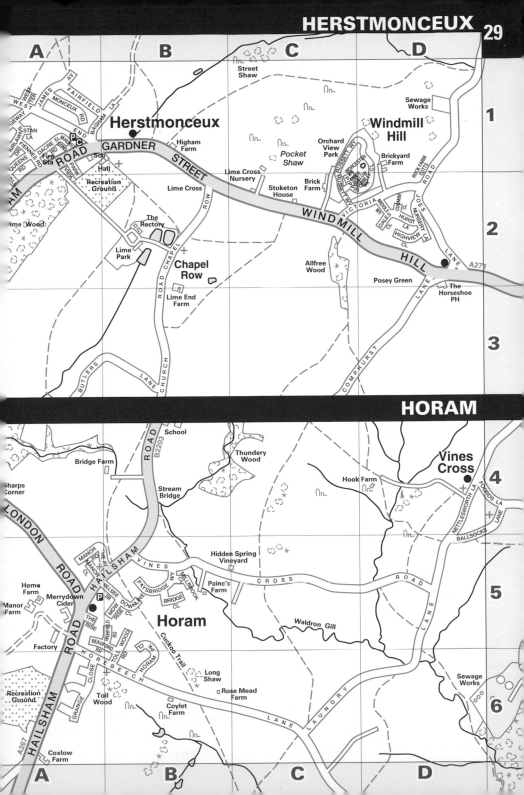

HERSTMONCEUX

A   **B**   **C**   **D**

Street Shaw

Sewage Works

WEST   AV   JAMES   FAIRFIELD   MONCEUX   RD   BAGHAM

Herstmonceux

Windmill Hill

Higham Farm

Pocket Shaw

Orchard View Park

Brickyard Farm

RICK FARM COTTS

ROAD

STAN LA

AIRLAWN   PIENNES   FIENNES   RD   DACRE   EL   MHRS   RD

QUEENS   RD

DR   RD

GARDNER   STREET   WINDMILL   HILL

Fire Sta   P   C

Sch

Hall

Recreation Ground

Lime Cross Nursery

Lime Cross

Stokaton House

Brick Farm

RUSSELL WY   WORCESTER   PIPPIN WY   RUSSELL WY   BRAMLEY   COX

VICTORIA   RD

ROW

COMBER   JOE'S NURSERY LA

JOE'S   LANE

Lime Wood

The Rectory

Lime Park

Chapel Row

CHAPEL   ROAD

Lime End Farm

Allfree Wood

Posey Green

COMPHURST LANE

VICTORIA LANE

MINNS   DALE'S   CL   HURST   LA   HIGHVIEW CL

A271

The Horseshoe PH

BUTLERS   LANE   CHURCH   LANE

1

2

3

HORAM

School

Thundery Wood

Hook Farm

Vines Cross

NETTLESWORTH LA   FOSROS LA   LANE

ROAD   B2203

Bridge Farm

Stream Bridge

BALLSOCKS

Sharps Corner

LONDON   ROAD

MANOR   THE   MANOR   RD   VINES

Hidden Spring Vineyard

CROSS   ROAD

Home Farm

Manor Farm

Merrydown Cider

P

PAYSBRIDGE   HILLSIDE   MILLBROOK   BRIDGE CL   MILL WY   DOWNLANE   RISE CL

Paine's Farm

Waldron Gill

LANE

Horam

THE RISE

BEAUFORD RD   HIGHFIELD RD   TOLL WOOD

HORSEBEECH   CLOSE   GRANGE   HORAM   RD

Cuckoo Trail

Long Shaw

Rose Mead Farm

LAUNDRY   LANE

Factory

Toll Wood

Coylet Farm

Recreation Ground

A267   HAILSHAM   ROAD

Coxlow Farm

Sewage Works

4

5

6

A   **B**   **C**   **D**

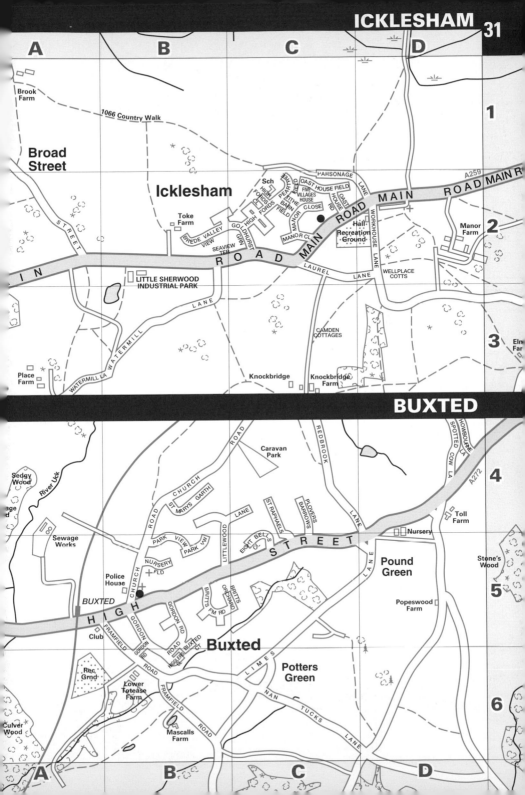

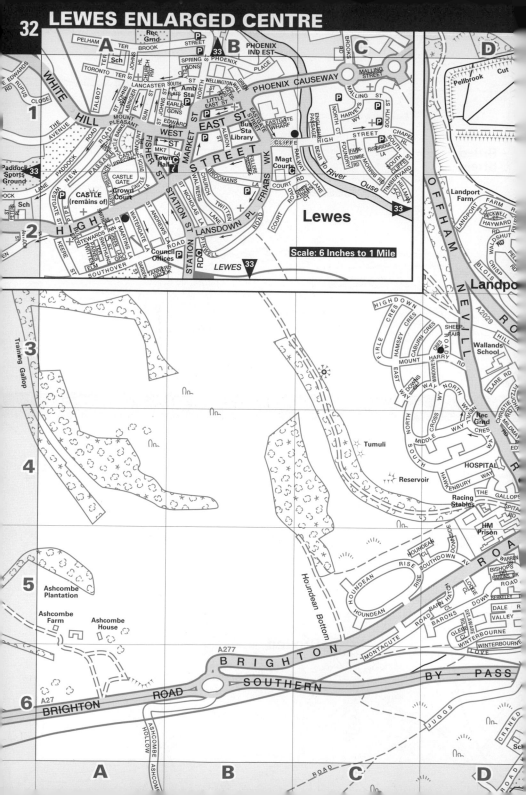

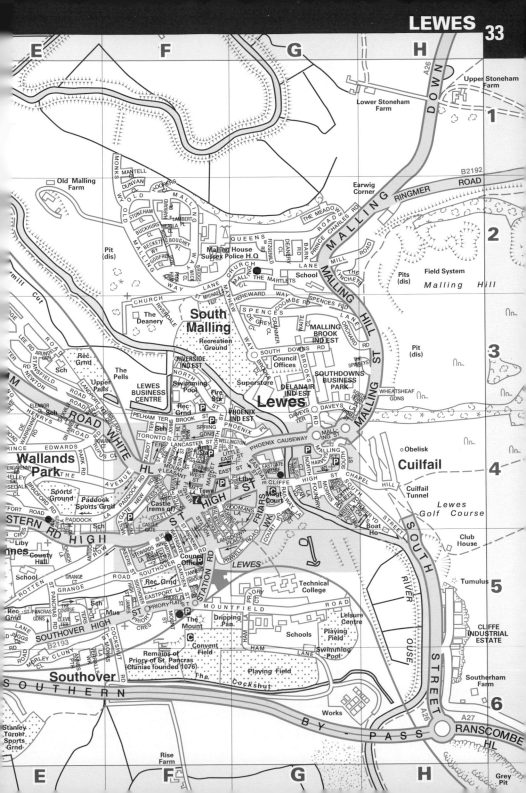

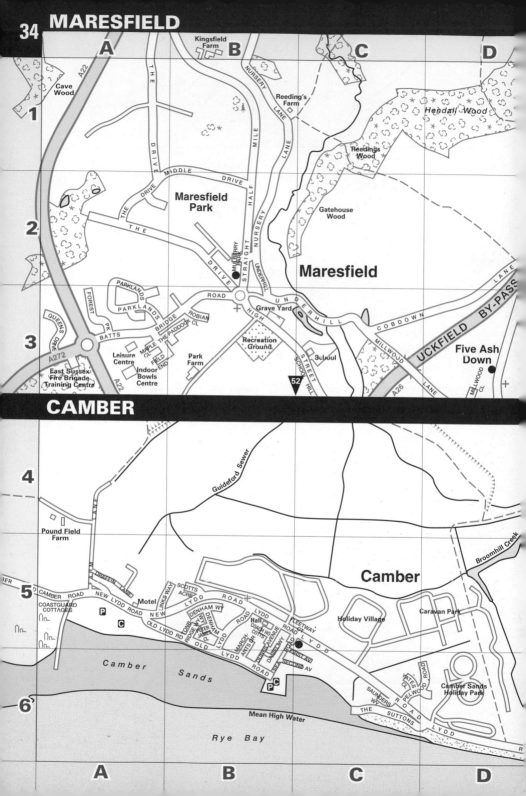

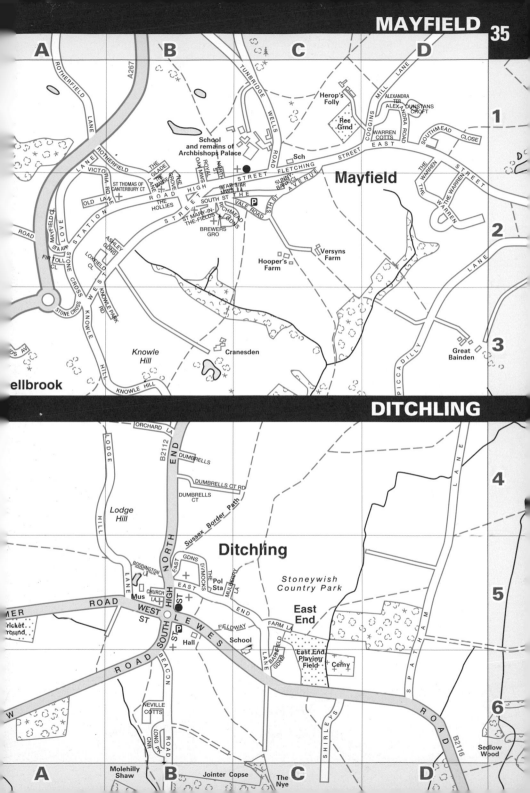

South Heighton

Denton

Mount Pleasant

Tarring Neville

Piddinghoe

RIVER OUSE

NEW ROAD

Manor Farm

Tarring Court Farm

Durham Farm

Brookside Farm

Caravan Park

Downs Villas

South Heighton Farm

Pages New Barn

New Barn

Snap Hill

Mount Pleasant Road

St Leonards Rd

The Close

Canterbury

St Leonards Cl

The Crescent

Fairholme Road

Seaview Road

Crest Road

Palmerste Road

Homedale Road

Falaise Road

Claremont Road

Arundel Road

Kings Avenue

Beresford Road

Denton Avenue

Harfield Cl

Rookery Rd

Lewis Rise

Thompson Rd

Park Dr

Denton Rise

Hill Rise

Denton Road

Wellington Road

Rectory Road

Guinness Trust

Port Bungalows

Acacia Cres

The Grove

Denton

Powell Rd

Ivegh Cres

St Martins

Crofts

Westview Ter

Tarring Cl

Heighton

Portland Ter

Hampden Gdns

Southview Ter

Glynde Cl

Beards

Forward Cl

Ivy Wy

School

Rec Grnd

Brookside

Shepherds

Court Farm Close

Cemy

Paradise Park

Euro Business Park

Willow Industrial Estate

Avis Way Industrial Estate

North

Station Road

B2109

B2109

A26

LEWES

STATION ROAD

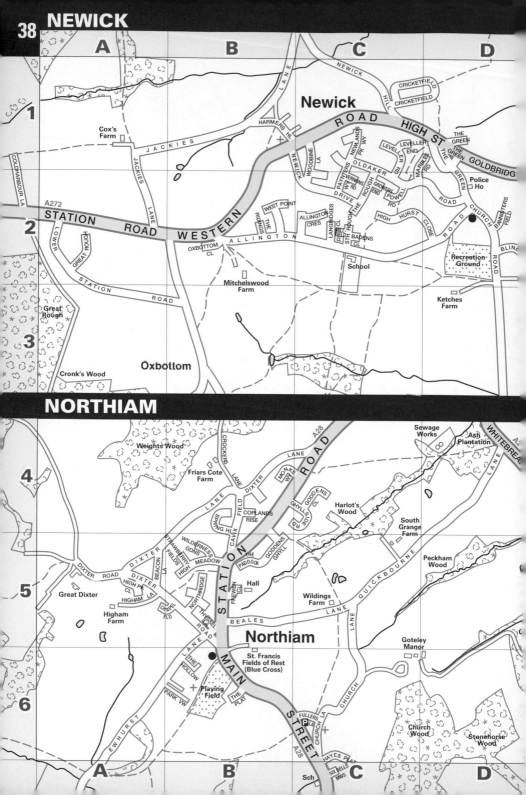

Peacehaven

Peacehaven Heights

Friar's Bay

Reservoir

Football Field

Reservoir

MERIDIAN IND EST

MERIDIAN CENTRE

Youth Centre

Meridian Leisure Centre

Liby

Sch

Chene Gap

Tumulus

Caravan Site

Motel

Friar's Bay

THE PROMENADE

Rec Gnd

Pal Sta

School

A259

A259

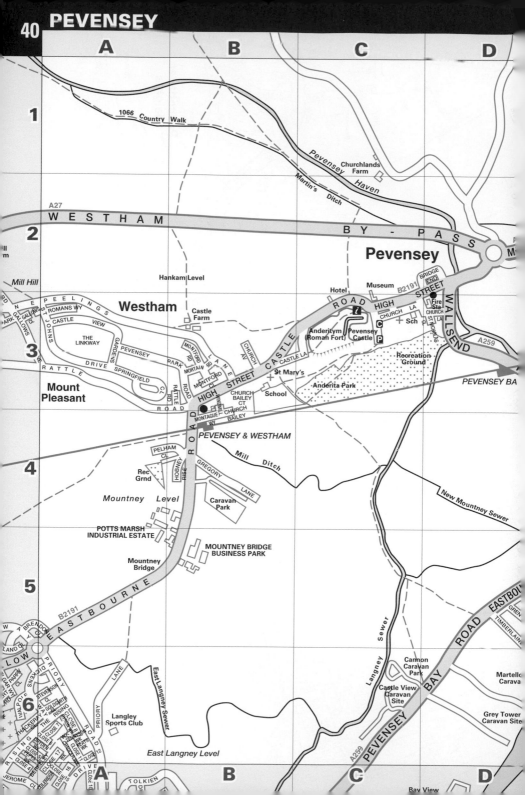

A   B   C   D

1

1066 Country Walk

Pevensey Haven

Churchlands Farm

Martin's Ditch

2

A27

W E S T H A M

B Y - P A S S

Pevensey

M

Mill Hill

Hankam Level

BRIDGE END

STREET

B2191

HIGH

WALLSEND

Hotel

Museum

Westham

Castle Farm

Fire Sta

CHURCH

CHURCH LA

Sch

ST NICHOLAS

A259

ROMANS WY

PEELINGS

CASTLE VIEW

JOHNS

GARDENS

PEVENSEY

PARK

3

THE LINKWAY

DRIVE SPRINGFIELD

RATTLE

MONTFORD

RD

MORTAIN

MONTFORD

LANE

ROAD

CHURCH AV

ROAD

CASTLE

HIGH STREET

Anderitvm (Roman Fort)

Pevensey Castle

Recreation Ground

PEVENSEY BA

CASTLE LA

St Mary's

Anderita Park

Mount Pleasant

RATTLE RD

WINDMILL

CHURCH BAILEY CT

School

CHURCH BAILEY

MONTAGUE WY

PEVENSEY & WESTHAM

4

PELHAM CL

GREGORY

Mill   Ditch

HONEY RISE

LANE

New Mountney Sewer

Rec Grnd

Mountney   Level

Caravan Park

POTTS MARSH INDUSTRIAL ESTATE

MOUNTNEY BRIDGE BUSINESS PARK

Mountney Bridge

EASTBOURNE

5

B2191

EASTBO

Langney Sewer

Cannon Caravan Park

Martello Carava

BRENDON CL

LAND CL

LOW

PRIORY

DICKENS

STEVENSON

EastLangney Sewer

Castle View Caravan Site

BAY

ROAD

Grey Tower Caravan Site

6

WALPOLE

PRIORY ROAD

RISING

Langley Sports Club

East Langney Level

A259

PEVENSEY

Bay View

JEROME

TOLKIEN

A   B   C   D

E **F** **G** **H**

A259

ROAD

Enclosure

d Haven

1

Nature *Reserve*

2

TOWER CL

UNTNEY DR

HAROLD CL

ARUNDEL CL

SQUARE

THE PARADE

SUNSET CL

BOULEVARD

WESTHAM

DRIVE

MARESFIELD

THE HAVEN CL

CAMBER CL

CAMBER DR

MARINE

MARINE AV

SOUTH CL

BEACHLANDS WAY

ROAD

BROADLAND WY

CAMBER

DRIVE

Pevensey *Bridge* *Level*

Beachlands

3

Pevensey Bay

SEND

ROAD

COBALD RD

PEBBLE

Park

GDNS

WAY

HAVEN

PRIORY CL

BAY AV

S CHANNEL

PARADE

WY RD

EASTBOURNE

SEAVILLE DR

MARINE RD

THE

T

DRIVE

NORTH

RICHMOND ROAD

COLLIER RD

HARRINGTON RD

SEA RD

P

RD

RD

RD

PC

LEYLAND RD

WESTERN RD

BAY

THE PROMENADE

P C

4

B *A* *Y*

BOURNE

ROSETTI RD

NORMAN RD

P *E* *V* *E* *N* *S* *E* *Y*

5

6

E **F** **G** **H**

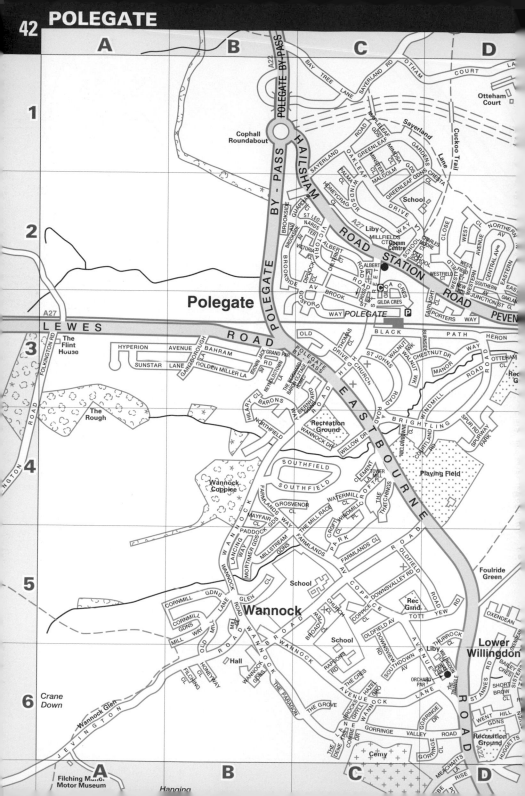

Portslade-by-Sea

Longhill High School

Rottingdean Place

New Barn

Rottingdean Youth Centre

Cricket & Football Ground

Playing Field

Playing Field

Tumuli

Beacon Hill

ST DUNSTANS REHABILITATION CENTRE

Miniature Golf Course

Windmill

Whipping Post

Liby & Museum

Sch

Rottingdean School

Rottingdean

Our Lady of Lourdes R.C.

St Aubyns Sch

Playing Field

St Aubyns Mead

Knole

Grand Park

The Park

St Margarets

St Tor Sta

Hall

Greenway Bottom

Under Cliff Walk

MARINE

DRIVE

FALMER ROAD

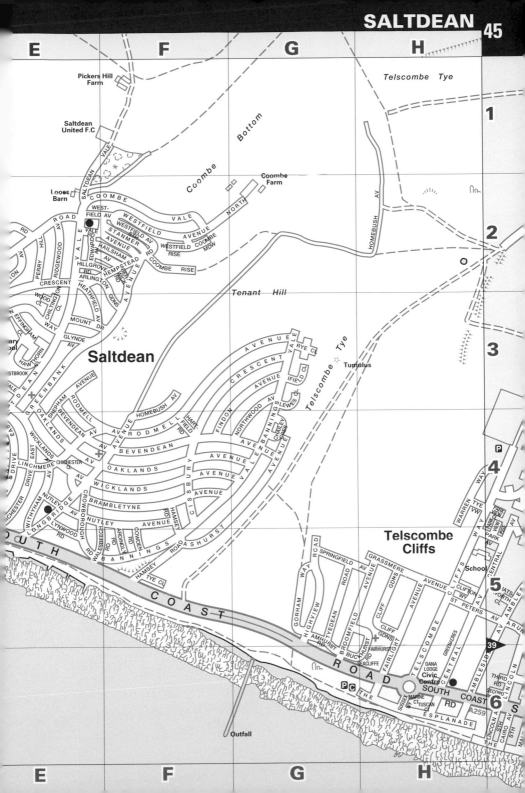

Saltdean

Telscombe Cliffs

Pickers Hill Farm

Telscombe Tye

Saltdean United F.C

Coombe Bottom

Coombe Farm

Loose Barn

Coombe North

Homebush AV

WESTFIELD VALE AVENUE
WEST-FIELD AV
STANMER RD
HAILSHAM
HILLGROVE RD
HEMPSTEAD RD
ARLINGTON GDNS
COOMBE MDW
COOMBE RISE
WESTFIELD RISE

PERRY HILL
RIDGEWOOD
WOOD CL
CHILTINGTON WAY
HEATHFIELD AV
MOUNT DR
GLYNDE AV
CRESCENT
EFFINGHAM
HAWTHORN
STBROOK

Tenant Hill

Telscombe Tye
Tumulus

RYE CL
VALE
IFIELD CL
CRESCENT AVENUE
AVENUE
LEWES CL
CHATLEY
SHERHAM
GREENBANK
RODMELL AV
BEVENDEAN AV
OAKLANDS
HOMEBUSH AV
RODMELL RD
HARTFIELD
FINDON
NORTHWOOD AV
BANNING AV
VALE
BEVENDEAN
WICKLANDS
CHICHESTER CL
LINCHMERE AV
DRIVE EAST
DRIVE
WICKLANDS
BRAMBLETYNE
CISBURY
AVENUE
AVENUE

WITHYHAM
NUTLEY
LONGRIDGE
LYNWOOD
CROWBOROUGH RD
NUTLEY AV
ARDINGLY RD
COWDEN RD
BANNINGS
HAMSEY
ASHURST
HAMSEY
TYE CL

SOUTH

COAST

Telscombe Cliffs

GORHAM WAY
HIGHVIEW
AMHURST
TYEDEAN RD
BROOMFIELD RD
BUCKHURST
SEACLIFFE
FAIRLIGHT
WALESBECH
SPRINGFIELD RD
GRASSMERE
CLIFF GDNS
CLIFF GDNS
FAIRHURST
TELSCOMBE
AVENUE
CLIFFS
CLIFTON WY
ST PETERS AV
GREENACRES
CENTRAL AV
AMBLESIDE AV
WARREN TYE VW
PARK VIEW
CENTRAL
School
WAY
ARUN

Dana Lodge
Civic Centre

Sussex Ct
MARINE CT
TUSCAN CT

THE
ESPLANADE

SOUTH COAST RD
A259

THIRD RD
SECOND
LINCOLN
CAIRO AV
STH

Outfall

39

Stud Farm

A B C D

1

Tumuli
Tumuli

Bishopstone Place (site of)

Rookery Hill

The Rookery

SILVER LANE

AVENUE

East Blatchingt

GLENEAGLES CL
HOLMES CL
TROON CL
EDWARD CL
ST ANDREWS
ELIZABETH CL
FREELAND CL
WINDSOR CL
ROSEMOUNT CL
MARGARETS RISE
HARBOUR CL
VIKING CL
ROMAN CL
HANOVER CL
NORMAN CL
ANTONY CL
ROCHFORD VW
HURDIS RD
SEAGRAVE CL
MARINE DRIVE

Bishopstone

ROOKERY WAY

BISHOPSTONE DRIVE

2

Mill
DROVE

SEAFORD RD
A259

NEWHAVEN ROAD

Tide Mills

37

HILL RISE

GRAND

BUCKLE BY-PASS

PRINCESS

BARONS

CLEMENTINE

CHURCHILL RD
PRINCESS
CLOSE
VICTOR
AUDREY
ELEANOR
KATHERINE
ISABEL
ALEXANDRA WA
REGE
PRINCESS

BEACON
CHARLES RD
DUKES DR
EARLS DR
TUDOR
KINGS RIDE
BUCKINGHAM CL
KINGS CL
CROSS WA
KINGSMEAD
REGE

3

Camping & Caravan Park

Motel

STATION RD

HAWTH CL
HAWTH HILL
HAWTH CRES
HAWTH PARK RD
HAWTH RD

MARINE

BISHOPSTONE

Sunnyside Caravan Site

BUCKLE DR
BUCKLE CL
BUCKLE RISE
BIDDLE DR

KINGSWAY

NEWHAVEN RD

BEACON RD

FRISTON CL
JEVINGTON DR
SURREY CL
BISHOPS CL

TUDOR

ROAD

BEACON
WESTDOWN RD
WILMINGTON RD
BELGRAVE RD
GROSVENOR RD
GROSVENOR
SALISBURY RD
CHIC
CLAREMO
RD

4

SEAFORD

PARADE

MARINE

KIMBERLEY RD
QUEENS PARK CL
SURREY CL

ALBANY RD
CLAREMONT RD
CONNAUGHT RD
BEAME CT
EDINBURGH RD
BEACH RD
PARK RD

CLAREMONT RD

SEAFORD STATION

St CRISPIANS RD

Salts Recreation Ground

Bus Depot

SEAFORD
He
Ce

DANE RD
DANE CL
GREEN LA
WEST VW
STRATHEDEN CT
MONO RD

Vanguard

5

BAY

PARADE

ESPLA

6

A B C D

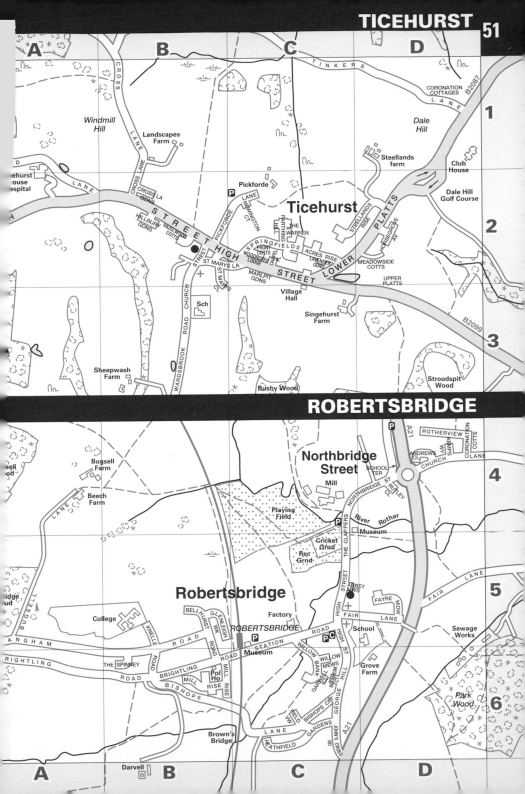

A B C D

1

Windmill Hill

Landscapes Farm

CORONATION COTTAGES

TINKERS

LANE

B2087

Dale Hill

Steellands farm

Club House

ehurst ouse ospital

CROSS LANE

LANE

CROSS LANE

CROSS LA GDNS

HILLBURY GDNS

IDGELWOOD COTTS

STREET HIGH

Pickforde

PICKFORDE LANE

ORINGTON CT

P

Ticehurst

THE WARREN

FARTHING HILL

Dale Hill Golf Course

STEELLANDS

PLATTS

2

SPRINGFIELDS

FRONT COTTS RD

WOODROYDE LODGE

FIELD

LAVENDER GDNS

ACRES RISE

STEELLANDS LA

HORSEGROVE AV

MEADOWSIDE COTTS

LOWER

STREET

ST MARYS LA

MARLPIT GDNS

STREET

ST MARYS

CHURCH ROAD

WARDSBROOK ROAD

Sch

Village Hall

UPPER PLATTS

3

B2099

Sheepwash Farm

Singehurst Farm

Bushy Wood

Stroodspit Wood

A21

ROTHERVIEW

Bugsell Farm

P

Northbridge Street

ANDREWS CL

CHURCH LANE

CORONATION COTTS

SCHOOL TER

NORTHBRIDGE ST

RUTLEY CL

4

sell od

Beech Farm

LANE

Mill

Playing Field

P

River Rother

Museum

BUGSELL

College

Cricket Grnd

Rec Grnd

THE CLAPPERS

HIGH STREET

5

idge od

Robertsbridge

BELLHURST

GLENLEIGH WK

KNELLE ROAD

ROAD

Factory

ROBERTSBRIDGE

ABBEY MDWS

FAYRE

FAIR LANE

MDW

FAIR LANE

FAIR LANE

Sewage Works

School

ANGHAM

RIGHTLING

THE SPINNEY

BRIGHTLING

MILL RISE

ROAD

BISHOPS

ROAD

Pol Ho

MILL RISE

P

Station Museum

WILLOW BANK

WILLOW MEWS

DARVELL

VW

BISHOPS CFT

GARDENS

GEORGE HILL

RD SCHOO

HIGH ST

A21

Grove Farm

Park Wood

6

Brown's Bridge

Darvell

EATHFIELD

LANE

A B C D

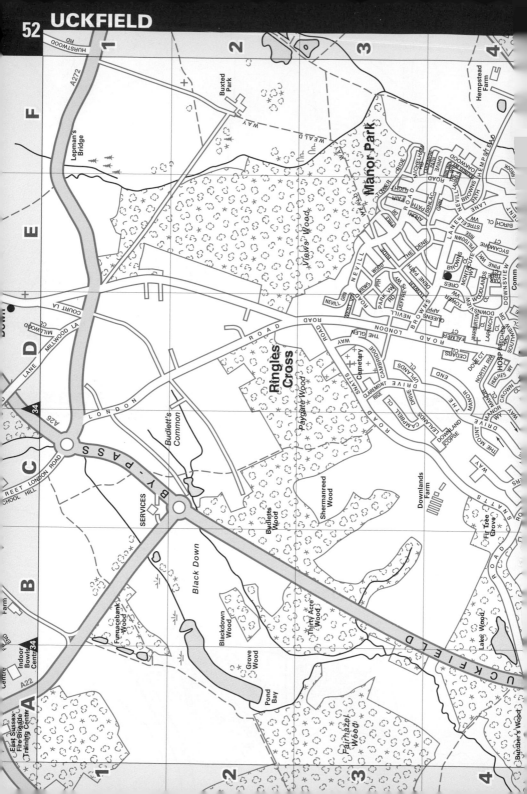

Black Down

Ringles Cross

Manor Park

Budlett's Common

Services

By-Pass

Buxted Park

Lepman's Bridge

Hempstead Farm

Furnacebank Wood

Blackdown Wood

Grove Wood

Pond Bay

Fairhazel Wood

Budletts Wood

Shermanreed Wood

Thirty Acre Wood

Downlands Farm

Fir Tree Grove

Lake Wood

Butcher's Wood

Views Wood

Paygate Wood

Cemetery

East Sussex Fire Brigade Training Centre

Indoor Bowls Centre

A272

A26

A22

HURSTWOOD RD

COURT LA

MILLWOOD LA

LANE

LONDON ROAD

SCHOOL HILL

LONDON ROAD

WEALD WAY

LONDON ROAD

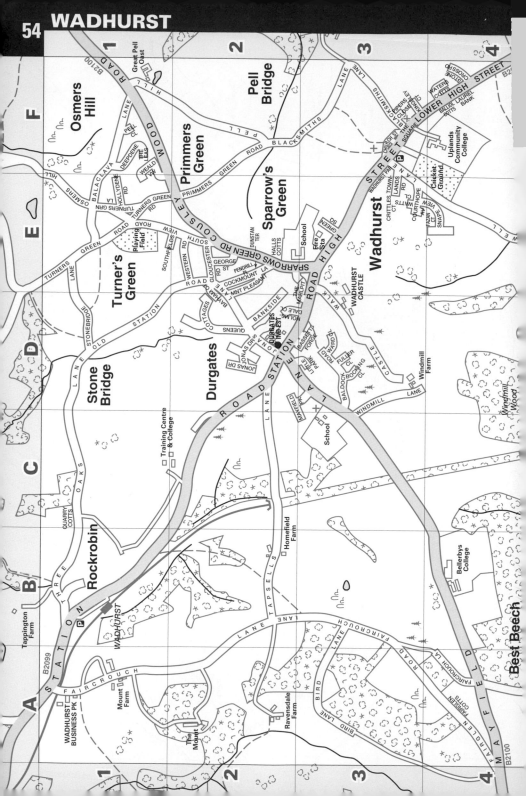

Osmers Hill

Great Pell Oast

Primmers Green

Pell Bridge

Sparrow's Green

Wadhurst

Uplands Community College

Cricket Ground

Lower High Street

School

Wadhurst Castle

Windmill Farm

Windmill Wood

Turner's Green

Playing Field

Stone Bridge

Durgates

Training Centre & College

School

Rockrobin

Tappington Farm

Wadhurst Business Pk

Mount Farm

The Mount

Homefield Farm

Ravensdale Farm

Bellerbys College

Best Beech

WADHURST

B2099

B2100

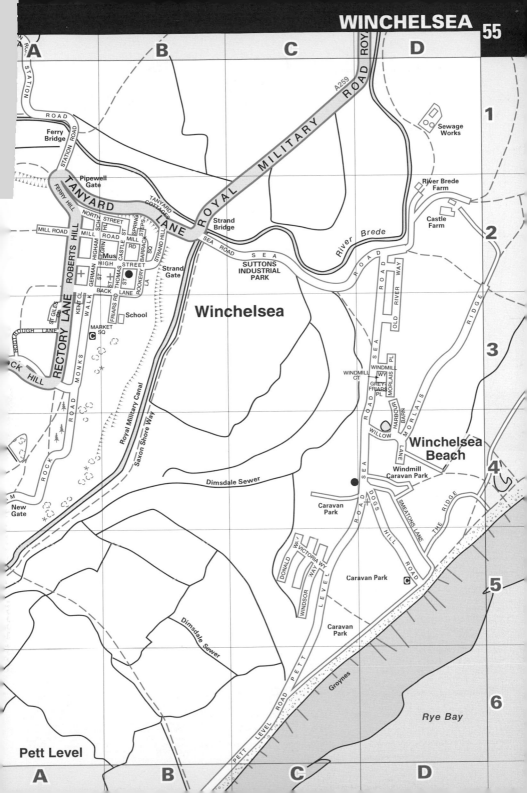

Winchelsea

Winchelsea Beach

Pett Level

Rye Bay

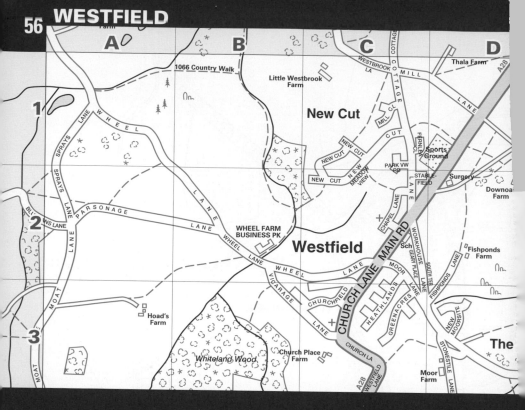

A - Z INDEX TO STREETS
with Postcodes

The Index includes some names for which there is insufficient space on the maps. These names are indicated by an * and are followed by the nearest adjoining thoroughfare.

Abbey Ct TN33 13 C3
Abbey Mews TN32 51 C5
Abbey Path BN27 24 E4
Abbey Rd BN20 20 A1
Abbey Vw TN40 15 E2
Abbey Way TN33 13 C3
Abbots Cl TN33 13 E4
Abbotsbury Cl BN2 44 D4
Abbotsfield Cl TN34 26 B2
Abergavenny Rd BN7 33 E4
Abinger Pl BN7 32 A1
Abinger Rd BN41 43 A3
Acacia Av BN3 30 A2
Acacia Rd BN9 36 E3
Acorn Grn BN27 24 D4
Acres Rise TN5 51 C2
Addingham Rd BN22 21 H1
Adelaide Cl BN25 48 D2
Adelaide Cres BN3 30 D6
Adelaide Mansions BN3 30 D6
Ainsworth Av BN22 44 A2
Air St BN1 16 D4
Albany Mews BN3 30 C5
Albany Rd, Bexhill TN40 14 D5
Albany Rd, St Leonards TN38 50 B4
Albany Rd, Seaford BN25 48 C4
Albany Villas BN3 30 C6
Albert Mews BN3 30 D5
Albert Par BN21 20 B1
Albert Pl BN26 42 C2
Albert Rd, Bexhill TN40 14 D5
Albert Rd, Brighton BN1 16 D1

Albert Rd, Hastings TN34 26 B5
Albert Rd, Polegate BN26 42 C2
Albert Rd, Uckfield TN22 53 D6
Albert Ter BN21 20 B1
Albion Hill BN2 17 G1
Albion Rd BN22 21 G1
Albion St, Brighton BN2 17 G2
Albion St, Lewes BN7 32 B1
Albion St, Portslade-by-Sea BN41 43 B5
Aldborough Rd TN37 50 C2
Alder Cl TN21 28 C4
Aldrington Av BN3 30 B3
Aldrington Cl BN3 43 D4
Alexandra Cl BN25 48 D2
Alexandra Rd, Heathfield TN21 28 D3
Alexandra Rd, Mayfield TN20 23 D1
Alexandra Rd, St Leonards TN37 50 C3
Alexandra Rd, Uckfield TN22 53 D6
Alexandra Ter TN20 23 D1
Alexandra Villas BN1 16 D1
Alford Way TN40 15 F3
Alfray Rd TN40 15 H3
Alfred Rd, Hastings TN35 27 E2
Alfred St TN38 50 C4
Alfriston Cl BN20 20 B3
Alfriston Pk BN25 49 H2
Alfriston Rd, Polegate BN26 12 A6
Alfriston Rd, Seaford BN25 49 F3
All Saints Cres TN34 26 D4
All Saints Gdns TN21 28 B2
All Saints La TN39 14 C1

All Saints St TN34 26 C5
Allen Way TN40 15 G2
Allington Cres BN8 38 C2
Allington Rd BN8 38 B2
Alma Ter TN37 50 C1
Alma Villas TN37 50 C1
Almonry Flds TN33 13 A3
Alpine Rd, Hastings TN34 26 C4
Alpine Rd, Hove BN3 30 A4
Amanda Cl TN40 15 G2
Amberley Dr BN3 30 A1
Amberstone Cl TN34 26 C1
Amberstone Vw BN27 24 E3
Ambleside Av BN10 39 A1
Amesbury Cres BN3 43 D4
Amherst Cl TN34 50 D2
Amherst Cres BN3 30 A3
Amherst Gdns TN34 50 D2
Amherst Rd, Bexhill TN40 14 C4
Amherst Rd, Hastings TN34 26 A4
Amherst Rd, St Leonards TN37 50 C2
Amhurst Rd BN10 45 G5
Anchor Ct BN8 47 B3
Anchor Fld BN8 47 B3
Anderida Rd BN22 42 D6
Anderson Cl BN9 37 A5
Andrews Cl TN32 51 D4
Angela Cl TN40 15 G2
Anglesea Ter TN38 50 C3
Anglesey Av BN27 24 B3
Ann St, Brighton BN1 17 F1
Ann St, Hastings TN34 26 D2
Annes Path BN7 33 E6
Antares Path BN27 25 F6
Antioch St BN7 33 E5
Antony Cl BN25 48 A2
Anvil Cl, Brighton BN41 43 A1
Anvil Cl, Uckfield TN22 53 C6
Ash Ct BN27 25 C6

Apex Pk BN27 25 C7
Apex Way BN27 25 C6
Applesham Av BN3 43 D1
Applesham Way BN41 43 A2
Aquarius Cl BN10 39 C3
Aquila Pk BN25 49 F4
Arbourvale TN38 50 A2
Archery Rd TN38 50 B4
Archery Walk BN27 25 E7
Ardingly Rd BN2 45 F5
Ardingly St BN2 17 G5
Argent Cl BN25 49 F2
Arlington Gdns BN2 45 E2
Arlington Rd BN21 21 E2
Arlington Rd East BN27 25 B7
Arlington Rd West BN27 25 A7
Arran Cl BN27 24 C4
Arthur Rd TN39 14 B4
Arthur St BN3 30 B3
Arun Path TN22 52 E3
Arundel Cl, Hailsham BN27 24 E3
Arundel Cl, Pevensey BN24 41 G2
Arundel Dr East BN2 45 E4
Arundel Dr West BN2 44 D4
Arundel Grn BN7 33 E3
Arundel Rd, Eastbourne BN21 21 E2
Arundel Rd, Newhaven BN9 36 E4
Arundel Rd, Peacehaven BN10 39 B2
Arundel Rd, Seaford BN25 49 G4
Arundel Rd Central BN10 39 B2
Arundel Rd West BN10 39 A1
Ascham Pl BN20 20 D4
Ascot Cl BN20 21 E5
Ascot Mews TN38 50 B3
Ash Ct BN27 25 C6

Ash Dr BN25
Ash Tree Cl TN21
Ash Walk BN9
Ashburnham Pl BN27
Ashburnham Rd, Eastbourne BN21
Ashburnham Rd, Hastings TN35
Ashby Cl TN39
Ashcombe Hollow BN7
Ashcroft Cl BN8
Ashdown Av BN2
Ashdown Cl RH18
Ashdown Ct TN6
Ashdown Pl TN21
Ashdown Rd, Bexhill TN40
Ashdown Rd, Forest Row RH18
Ashenden Av TN31
Ashford Cl BN27
Ashford Rd, Eastbourne BN21
Ashford Rd, Hastings TN35
Ashford Sq BN21
Ashford Way TN34
Ashington Gdns BN10
Ashlands TN6
Ashleigh Gdns TN6
Ashley Gdns, Hailsham BN27
Ashley Gdns, Mayfield TN20
Ashlings Way BN3
Ashton Rise BN2
Ashtonville Cl BN8
Ashurst Av BN2
Ashurst Rd BN25
Aspen Walk TN21
Asten Flds TN33
Athelstan Rd TN35

St BN2	17 H6
TN39	14 D2
N25	48 D2
N21	21 E2
N21	21 F2
TN6	18 B4
	36 E4
	36 D3
9	36 D4
BN27	25 C6
9	
BN22	21 G1
,	
's TN38	50 A2
,	
N25	49 E4
N3	30 B5
6	55 A2
N8	38 C2
N41	43 A1
e TN31	46 B3
ough TN6	18 C3
n BN9	37 C7
opse BN25	49 H4
BN27	29 A1
d BN26	42 B3
s BN22	42 D6
s Cl BN25	49 E5
N34	26 A2
N37	50 C3
en BN9	37 D6
Uckfield TN22	53 D6
BN21	20 D2
Rd BN21	20 C1
La TN5	54 E1
Rd BN10	39 A1
d TN5	54 D3
Rd TN34	26 B3
dns RH18	22 C4
BN8	47 D1
tts TN5	54 F4
La TN21	29 D5
Cl BN25	49 F2
d St BN41	43 A3
Ho TN39	14 C3
Rd TN39	14 C3
N39	14 D2
, Rye TN31	46 B3
, Wadhurst TN5	54 D2
Vale BN2	45 E5
s Fld BN8	38 D2
e Cl BN25	49 H5
e Cl,	
urne BN20	20 B2
e Cl,	
n BN25	49 H6
e Walk BN20	20 B2
d BN22	21 H1
Cl TN39	14 D2
y TN35	27 E4
a TN35	26 D4
Hailsham BN27	24 D4
Seaford BN25	49 G2
ch Cl BN7	32 D5
BN7	33 G2
e BN25	49 F2
Rd BN41	43 A3
Way TN22	53 E5
d TN6	19 E4
d Cl TN34	50 D3
d Gdns BN6	35 C6
Cl BN25	48 C3
Down Rd BN7	32 D5
Walk BN7	32 D5
Way BN26	42 B3
Rd TN40	14 D4
Sq TN36	55 D2
mew Sq BN1	17 E5
mews BN1	17 E5
d North BN41	43 A5
d South BN41	43 A5
Rd BN20	20 C6
s Forge TN5	54 D2
or Way TN22	53 B5
BN21	21 E3
BN1	16 C1
Hill TN35	23 A3
BN25	49 H2
Cres BN27	25 D5
Gates TN33	13 A3
Hill TN33	13 E4
Rd,	
ham BN27	25 D5
nfield TN21	28 E1
Rd,	
onards TN37	50 B1
ridge Rd TN22	53 B1
Rd BN7	33 E3
BN24	41 F4

Bay Pond Rd BN21	20 C1
Bay Rd BN24	41 E5
Bay Tree Cl TN21	28 D4
Bay Tree La BN26	42 C1
Bay Vue Rd BN9	37 C6
Bayencourt North TN40	14 C4
Bayencourt South TN40	14 C4
Bayham Ct TN5	54 D2
Bayham Rd, Eastbourne BN22	21 H2
Bayham Rd, Hailsham BN27	25 E6
Bayview Rd BN10	39 E4
Bazehill Rd BN2	44 B3
Beach Cl, Newhaven BN9	37 D6
Beach Cl, Seaford BN25	48 C4
Beach Rd BN9	37 D6
Beachlands Way BN24	41 G3
Beachy Head Rd BN20	20 B6
Beacon Cl, Crowborough TN6	18 C4
Beacon Cl, Seaford BN25	48 D3
Beacon Dr BN25	48 D3
Beacon Gdns TN6	18 C3
Beacon Hill, Bexhill TN39	14 A1
Beacon Hill, Brighton BN2	44 A2
Beacon La TN31	38 A5
Beacon Rd, Crowborough TN6	18 A6
Beacon Rd, Hassocks BN6	35 B6
Beacon Rd, Hastings TN35	27 F1
Beacon Rd, Seaford BN25	48 C4
Beacon Rd West TN6	18 B4
Beaconsfield Rd, Bexhill TN40	14 D3
Beaconsfield Rd, Brighton BN41	43 A3
Beaconsfield Rd, Hastings TN34	26 B3
Beales La TN31	38 B5
Beame Ct BN25	48 C4
Beamsley Rd BN22	21 H1
Bear Yd BN7	32 C1
Beatrice La BN21	21 E2
Beatrice Walk TN39	14 B3
Beauford Rd TN21	29 A5
Beaufort Cres TN37	50 C1
Beaufort Ter TN37	50 C1
Beaulieu Ct TN40	15 G4
Beaver Cl TN6	19 E5
Beckenham Cl BN27	24 D3
Becket Cl TN34	26 B4
Beckett Way TN7	33 F2
Bedford Av TN40	15 E5
Bedford Ct TN22	52 D4
Bedford Gro BN21	21 E1
Bedford Pl, Brighton BN1	16 A4
Bedford Pl, Rye TN31	46 C3
Bedford Rd, Uckfield TN22	53 D5
Bedford Rd TN35	27 E2
Bedford Sq BN1	16 A4
Bedfordwell Rd BN21	21 E1
Bee Rd BN10	39 C1
Beech Cl TN33	13 B1
Beeches Cl, Heathfield TN21	28 D1
Beeches Cl, Uckfield TN22	52 D4
Beeches Farm Rd TN22	19 E5
Beeches Rd TN6	19 E5
Beeching Cl TN39	14 C4
Beeching Rd TN39	14 C5
Beechwood Cl BN27	25 D8
Beechwood Cres BN20	20 C2
Beechwood La TN21	28 D4
Beechy Av BN20	20 B1
Beechy Gdns BN20	20 A1
Belfast St BN3	30 C5
Belfry Orch TN52	53 D7
Belgrave Cres BN25	49 E2
Belgrave Rd BN25	48 D4
Belgrave St BN2	17 G2
Bell La, Lewes BN7	33 E5
Bell La, Uckfield TN22	53 B6
Bellbanks Rd BN27	25 D7
Belle Hill TN40	14 D4
Bellfarm Rd TN22	53 B5
Bellhurst Rd TN32	51 B5
Bellingham Cres BN3	43 C3
Belmont Rd, Hastings TN35	26 D4
Belmont Rd, Uckfield TN22	53 C5
Belmont St BN1	17 F1
Belmore Rd BN22	21 G1

Beltring Rd BN22	21 G1
Beltring Ter BN22	21 G1
Belvedere Gdns, Crowborough TN6	19 E6
Belvedere Rd, Seaford BN25	49 F2
Belvedere Pk TN38	50 A3
Bembrook Rd TN34	26 C4
Benenden Cl BN25	49 G3
Benenden Rise TN34	26 A1
Benett Av BN3	30 C1
Benett Dr BN3	30 C1
Benfield Cl BN41	43 B3
Benfield Cres BN41	43 B2
Benfield Way BN41	43 B2
Benson Ct BN3	43 D4
Beresford Rd BN9	36 D4
Beristede Cl BN20	21 E4
Berkeley Row BN7	33 G3
Berlin Rd TN35	27 E2
Bernard La BN21	21 E2
Bernhard Gdns BN26	42 C4
Berriedale Av BN3	30 B3
Berwick Cl BN25	48 C3
Berwick Rd BN2	45 F2
Bethune Rd TN40	15 E5
Bethune Way TN34	26 B4
Beuzeville Av BN27	25 D5
Bevendean Av BN2	45 E3
Bexhill Rd TN38,40	15 H4
Bexleigh Av TN38	15 H4
Bexley Cl BN27	24 C4
Bidwell Av TN39	14 B2
Birch Cl, Heathfield TN21	28 D3
Birch Cl, Uckfield TN22	52 E4
Birch Vw TN39	14 C2
Birch Way, Hailsham BN27	25 D8
Birch Way, Hastings TN34	26 A2
Birch Way, Heathfield TN21	28 D2
Birches Cl TN6	18 D2
Bird In Eye Hill TN22	53 E6
Bird La TN5	54 A3
Birling Cl BN25	48 C3
Birling Rd BN21	20 B1
Birling Way TN22	52 F4
Bishops Cft TN32	51 C6
Bishops Cl, Seaford BN25	48 C4
Bishops Dr BN7	32 D5
Bishops La, Lewes BN8	47 A2
Bishops La, Robertsbridge TN32	51 B6
Bishops Rd BN3	30 D2
Bishops Walk, Bexhill TN40	15 G2
Bishops Walk, Brighton BN1	16 C3
Bishopstone Dr BN2	44 D2
Bishopstone Rd BN25	48 B2
Black Lion La BN1	17 E5
Black Lion St BN1	17 E5
Black Path BN26	42 C3
Blackfields Av TN39	14 A3
Blacklands Cres RH18	22 D3
Blacklands Dr TN34	26 B2
Blackman St BN1	17 F1
Blackmill Cl TN39	14 B1
Blackness TN6	19 E5
Blackness Rd TN6	18 D5
Blacksmiths Copse BN27	25 C7
Blacksmiths La TN5	54 F2
Blackthorn Cl BN41	43 A1
Blackthorn Way TN35	23 D3
Blackwater Rd BN20	21 E4
Blakeney Av BN10	39 F3
Blaker St BN2	17 G4
Blatchington Cl BN25	49 E3
Blatchington Hill BN25	49 E3
Blatchington Rd, Hove BN3	30 C4
Blatchington Rd, Seaford BN25	48 D4
Blenheim Ct TN32	51 C6
Blenheim Flds RH18	22 B2
Blenheim Pl BN1	17 F3
Blind La BN8	38 D2
Blois Rd BN7	32 D2
Blomfield Rd TN37	50 D3
Blossom Walk BN27	24 D4
Blue Haze Av BN25	49 G3
Bocking Cl TN5	54 D3
Boddington La BN6	35 B5
Bodiam Av TN40	15 E2
Bodiam Cl BN25	49 H4
Bodle Cres TN39	14 C2
Bodmin Cl BN20	20 B2
Bohemia Rd, Hastings TN34	26 A5

Bohemia Rd, St Leonards TN37	50 C2
Bolebrook Rd TN40	15 E5
Bolney Av BN10	39 C3
Bolsover Rd, Eastbourne BN20	21 E5
Bolsover Rd, Hove BN3	30 A4
Bolton Rd BN21	21 F3
Bond St BN1	17 E4
Bond Street Cotts BN1	17 E4
Bond Street Row BN1	17 E4
Booker Cl TN6	19 E5
Borough La BN20	20 D2
Borough St BN1	16 A3
Boscobel Cl TN38	50 A5
Boscobel Rd TN38	50 A4
Boscobel Rd North TN38	50 A4
Boughey Pl BN7	33 F2
Boundary Rd BN3	43 C4
Bounds Way TN22	52 F4
Bourne Pass*, The Bourne TN34	26 C5
Bourne St BN21	21 F2
Bowden Rise BN25	49 E2
Bowley Rd BN27	25 E7
Bowmans Dr TN33	13 C2
Bowrey Pl TN40	14 C4
Boxgrove Cl TN40	15 G4
Boyces St BN1	16 D4
Boyne Rd TN35	27 E3
Bracken Cl TN6	19 G5
Bracken Rd BN25	49 G5
Brackenbury Cl BN41	43 A1
Brackendale TN35	27 F2
Bradford Rd BN7	33 E4
Bradford St BN21	20 C2
Brading Cl TN34	26 A3
Braemore Rd BN3	30 A5
Bramber Av BN10	39 B3
Bramber Av North BN10	39 C1
Bramber Cl, Peacehaven BN10	39 C1
Bramber Cl, Seaford BN25	49 E5
Bramber La BN25	49 E5
Bramber Rd BN25	49 E5
Bramble Cft TN6	19 E4
Bramble Dr BN27	25 C6
Bramble Way TN35	23 D4
Brambledean Rd BN41	43 A4
Brambleside TN22	53 B5
Brambletyne Av BN2	45 E4
Bramley Walk BN27	29 D2
Brampton Av TN39	14 A5
Brampton Ct TN39	14 A5
Brands Cl BN27	36 D3
Branksome Rd TN38	50 A3
Brassey Rd TN40	14 D5
Braybrooke Cl TN34	26 A5
Braybrooke Rd TN34	26 A5
Braybrooke Ter TN34	26 A5
Brazen Cl BN9	37 A6
Bread St BN1	17 E3
Brede Valley Vw TN36	31 B2
Brendon Rise TN34	26 D2
Brett Dr TN40	15 G4
Brewers Gro TN20	23 B1
Brewery Yd TN33	13 C3
Briar Cl TN35	23 E2
Brickmead TN6	19 E5
Bridge Cl TN21	29 B5
Bridge End BN24	40 C2
Bridge Farm Rd TN22	53 C6
Bridge Pl TN31	46 C3
Bridge St TN31	37 G5
Bridger Way TN6	18 D5
Bridgewick Cl BN7	33 F2
Brightland Rd BN20	20 C2
Brightling Av TN35	27 F1
Brightling Rd, Polegate BN26	42 C4
Brightling Rd, Robertsbridge TN32	51 A6
Brighton Pl BN1	17 E5
Brighton Rd, Lewes BN7	32 A6
Brighton Rd, Newhaven BN9	37 A6
Brighton Sq BN1	17 E4
Brills La BN1	17 F5
Brincliffe TN6	18 C3
Brittany Rd, Hove BN3	43 C5
Brittany Rd, St Leonards TN38	50 B4
Britts Farm Rd TN22	31 B5
Britts Orch TN22	31 B5
Broad Rd BN20	42 B5
Broad St, Brighton BN2	17 G5
Broad St, Seaford BN25	49 E5
Broad St, Winchelsea TN36	31 A1
Broad Vw TN39	14 A3
Broadoak La TN39	14 A3
Broadstone RH18	22 D3

Broadview Cl BN20	42 C5
Broadway, Crowborough TN6	18 D3
Broadway, Hastings TN35	23 D3
Brockley Rd TN39	14 B5
Brocks Ghyll BN20	42 C6
Brodie Pl BN21	20 D2
Bromley Rd BN25	49 G3
Brook Cl TN6	19 G5
Brook St, Hastings TN34	26 B4
Brook St, Lewes BN7	33 F4
Brook St, Polegate BN26	42 C3
Brook Ter TN6	18 B2
Brook Vw TN6	18 B2
Brooker Pl BN3	30 C5
Brooker St BN3	30 C5
Brookfield Rd TN40	15 F5
Brookland Cl, Hastings TN34	26 B3
Brookland Cl, Pevensey BN24	41 G3
Brooklyn Rd BN25	48 D4
Brooks Cl, Lewes BN7	33 G3
Brooks Cl, Newhaven BN9	37 C6
Brooks Rd BN7	33 G3
Brookside, Newhaven BN9	36 A2
Brookside, Uckfield TN22	53 B6
Brookside Av BN26	42 B2
Broomans La BN7	32 B1
Broomfield Av BN10	45 G6
Broomfield St BN20	20 B1
Broomgrove Rd TN34	26 C3
Brown Jack Av BN26	42 B3
Browning Rd BN21	28 C2
Browns Cl TN22	52 E4
Browns La TN22	52 D3
Browns Path TN22	52 E4
Broyle Cl BN8	47 D1
Broyle La BN8	47 D1
Broyle Paddock BN8	47 D1
Broyleside BN8	47 D2
Brunswick Rd BN3	16 A3
Brunswick Row BN1	17 F1
Brunswick St East BN3	16 A4
Brunswick Ter BN3	16 A4
Bryants Fields TN6	18 C3
Buckholt Av TN40	15 G2
Buckholt La TN39	14 D1
Buckhurst Cl BN7	33 F2
Buckhurst Pl TN39	14 C5
Buckhurst Rd, Bexhill TN40	14 D5
Buckhurst Rd, Peacehaven BN10	45 G6
Buckingham Cl, Brighton BN1	16 D1
Buckingham Cl, Seaford BN25	48 D3
Buckingham Rd BN1	16 D2
Buckingham St BN1	16 D2
Buckland Rd BN25	49 F3
Buckle By-Pass BN25	48 B3
Buckle Cl BN25	48 B4
Buckle Dr BN25	48 B4
Buckle Rise BN25	48 B4
Buckler St BN41	43 A3
Buckthorn Cl BN25	49 H4
Buckwell Ct BN7	32 D2
Buckwell Rise BN27	29 A1
Bugsell La TN32	51 A6
Bull La BN7	32 A2
Buller Cl TN6	19 E5
Bullfinch Gdns TN22	53 E7
Burdett Rd TN6	19 G5
Burfield Rd BN22	21 G2
Burhill Way TN38	50 A4
Burlington Gdns BN41	43 B2
Burlington Pl BN21	21 F3
Burlington Rd BN21	21 G3
Burnes Vale BN2	44 B3
Burnside BN26	42 B3
Burrow Down BN20	20 A1
Burton Walk BN27	25 D6
Burton Way TN38	50 B5
Burwash Rd TN21	28 D1
Bush Cottage Cl BN41	43 B1
Bush Rd BN9	36 A4
Bushy Cft TN39	14 A3
Bushyfields BN27	25 C6
Butlers La BN27	29 A3
Butts Fld BN27	25 E7
Buxted Ct TN22	31 B6
Buxton Dr TN39	14 C3
Buxton Rd BN20	20 D5
Bydown BN25	49 F4
Byfields Cft TN39	14 A3
Byron St BN3	30 B4
Byron Walk BN23	40 A6

Caburn Cres BN7 32 C3
Caburn Way BN27 25 C7
Cacklebury Cl BN27 25 C7
Cadborough Cliff TN31 46 A4
Cairo Av BN10 39 A2
Cairo Av South BN10 39 A2
Caisters Cl BN3 30 D3
Caldbec Ct TN33 13 C2
Caldbec Hill TN33 13 C2
Calgary Rd TN39 14 C2
Callums Walk TN40 15 F3
Calverley Rd BN21 21 E3
Calverley Walk BN21 21 E3
Calvert Cl TN22 53 B5
Calvert Rd, Hastings TN34 26 C3
Calvert Rd, Uckfield TN22 53 B5
Camber Cl, Pevensey BN24 41 G3
Camber Dr BN24 41 G3
Camber Rd, Camber TN31 34 A5
Camber Rd, Rye TN31 46 F3
Camber Way BN24 41 G3
Cambridge Gdns TN34 26 A5
Cambridge Gro BN3 30 D4
Cambridge Rd, Bexhill TN40 14 D3
Cambridge Rd, Eastbourne BN22 21 G1
Cambridge Rd, Hastings TN34 26 A5
Cambridge Rd, Hove BN3 16 A3
Cambridge Way TN22 52 D3
Camden Rd BN21 21 E3
Camden Cotts TN36 31 C3
Camden St BN41 43 B5
Camden Ter BN1 17 E2
Camelford St BN2 17 G5
Cameron Cl BN2 25 C5
Campbell Cl TN22 52 C3
Campbell Cl TN38 50 A3
Camperdown St TN39 14 B1
Canada Way TN39 14 C2
Cannon Pl BN1 16 C5
Cantelupe Rd TN40 15 F3
Canterbury Rise TN34 26 A1
Cantercrow Hill BN9 36 F3
Canute Rd TN35 27 E2
Capel Av BN10 39 C3
Capella Path BN27 25 F6
Caple Ct TN38 50 B3
Caple Gdns TN38 50 B4
Card Hill RH18 22 C4
Cardiff Rd TN38 50 C4
Cardinals Cl TN40 15 G2
Carew Rd BN21 20 D1
Carfax Cl TN39 14 C1
Carisbrooke Rd TN38 50 B4
Carlisle Par TN34 26 A6
Carlisle Rd, Eastbourne BN20 20 C5
Carlisle Rd, Hove BN3 30 A5
Carlton Cl BN25 48 D3
Carlton Hill BN2 17 G3
Carlton Pl BN2 17 H4
Carlton Rd, Eastbourne BN22 21 H1
Carlton Rd, Seaford BN25 48 D2
Carlton Ter BN41 43 C3
Caroline Cl BN25 48 C2
Carpenters Way BN27 25 C7
Carriers Path BN27 25 D6
Caspian Sq BN2 44 B3
Castle Banks BN7 32 A1
Castle Ditch La BN7 32 A2
Castle Dr BN24 41 E5
Castle Gate BN7 32 A2
Castle Gdns*,
Castle Hill Rd TN34 26 B5
Castle Hill Pass TN34 26 B5
Castle Hill Rd TN34 26 B5
Castle La BN24 40 B3
Castle Precinct BN7 33 F4
Castle Precincts BN7 32 A2
Castle Rd BN24 40 B3
Castle Rise, Lewes BN7 32 A1
Castle Rise, Uckfield TN22 53 D8
Castle Sq BN1 17 F5
Castle St, Brighton BN1 16 B4
Castle St, Winchelsea TN36 55 B2
Castle St*, Albert Rd TN34 26 B5
Castle View Gdns BN24 40 A3
Castle Walk TN5 54 D3
Castle Way TN22 53 E8
Castledown Av TN34 26 B5
Castleross Rd BN24 41 E5

Cavell Av BN10 39 B2
Cavell Av North BN10 39 B1
Cavendish Av, Eastbourne BN22 21 G2
Cavendish Av, St Leonards TN38 50 A4
Cavendish Mews BN3 16 A3
Cavendish Pl, Brighton BN1 16 B4
Cavendish Pl, Eastbourne BN21 21 F2
Cavendish Pl, Hastings TN34 26 C5
Cavendish St TN34 17 G5
Caves Rd TN38 50 A5
Cavix Fld TN31 38 B5
Cedars Cl TN32 52 D4
Cedarwell Cl BN9 36 A3
Celandine Dr TN38 50 A2
Central Av, Peacehaven BN10 39 A1
Central Av, Peacehaven BN10 45 H6
Central Av, Polegate BN26 42 D2
Centurion Rd BN1 16 D2
Ceylon Pl BN21,22 21 G2
Chaffinch Walk TN22 53 E7
Chailey Av BN2 44 C3
Chailey Cres BN2 45 G4
Chain La TN33 13 B2
Challoners Cl BN2 44 B3
Challoners Mews BN2 44 B3
Chalvington Cl BN25 49 F1
Chamberlain Rd BN21 20 B1
Chamberlaines La BN8 47 D2
Chandler Rd TN4 14 D6
Channel View Rd BN24 41 F4
Channel Vw TN40 14 D6
Channel Vw West TN40 14 D6
Channel Way TN35 23 C4
Chantry Av TN40 14 D3
Chantry La TN40 14 D4
Chapel Barn Cl BN27 25 E6
Chapel Cl BN25 49 E3
Chapel Cotts TN33 13 D4
Chapel Fld TN31 38 A5
Chapel Hill BN7 32 C1
Chapel La, Forest Row RH18 22 D3
Chapel La, Hastings TN35 56 C2
Chapel Mews BN3 16 A4
Chapel Park Rd TN37 50 C3
Chapel Pl, Brighton BN41 43 B4
Chapel Pl, Wadhurst TN5 51 C2
Chapel Rd BN41 43 A4
Chapel Row BN27 29 B2
Chapel St, Newhaven BN9 37 C5,6
Charity Farm Way TN6 19 E3
Charles Cl BN25 49 E3
Charles Moore Ct BN26 42 C2
Charles Rd TN38 50 B3
Charles Rd West TN38 50 B3
Charles St BN2 17 G5
Charleston Rd BN21 20 C1
Charlotte St BN2 17 H6
Charlston Av BN9 37 A7
Chartfield BN3 30 B1
Chartres Cl TN40 15 E3
Chartwell Cl BN25 48 D2
Chatham Pl BN25 48 D5
Chatham Rd TN37 50 C1
Chatsworth Cl BN10 39 A1
Chatsworth Gdns BN20 21 E5
Chaucer Walk BN23 40 A6
Chawbrook Rd BN22 21 G1
Cheapside BN1 17 E1
Chelsea Cl TN40 15 E4
Chelsea Mews*, North St TN37 50 C4
Chelston Av BN3 30 A3
Cheltenham Pl BN1 17 F3
Chene Av BN10 39 F3
Chepbourne Rd TN40 14 C4
Chequer Grange RH18 22 C4
Chequers Cl TN6 19 E4
Chequers Way TN6 19 E4
Cherry Garden Rd BN20 20 A2
Cherry Gdns TN21 28 A4
Cherry Tree Cl BN25 49 G2
Cherry Tree Gdns TN40 15 G2
Cherryside BN27 25 C6
Cherwell Rd TN21 28 B1
Chesterfield Gdns BN20 20 D5
Chesterfield Rd BN20 20 D5
Chesterton Av BN25 49 G4
Chesterton Dr BN25 49 G4

Chestnut Cl, Hailsham BN27 24 C4
Chestnut Cl, Herstmonceux BN27 29 A1
Chestnut Dr BN26 42 C3
Chestnut Way BN9 37 B6
Chichester Cl, Bexhill TN39 14 B2
Chichester Cl, Brighton BN2 45 E4
Chichester Cl, Peacehaven BN10 39 E2
Chichester Cl, Seaford BN25 49 E4
Chichester Dr East BN2 45 E4
Chichester Dr West BN2 44 D4
Chichester Dr West BN2 45 E4
Chichester Rd, St Leonards TN38 50 B1
Chichester Rd, Seaford BN25 48 D4
Chiltern Ct BN26 42 C4
Chiltern Dr TN34 26 D2
Chiltington Cl BN2 45 E3
Chiltington Way BN2 45 E3
Chiswick Pl BN21 21 F3
Chorley Av BN2 44 D3
Christie Av BN8 47 A2
Christie Rd BN7 32 D4
Christine Cl TN40 15 G2
Church App TN21 28 F4
Church Av BN24 40 B3
Church Bailey BN24 40 B4
Church Bailey Ct BN24 40 B3
Church Cl BN20 42 C5
Church Hill, Lewes BN8 47 A3
Church Hill, Newhaven BN9 37 B6
Church La, Eastbourne BN21 20 C2
Church La, Hailsham BN27 24 B1
Church La, Hassocks BN6 35 B5
Church La, Hastings TN35 56 C3
Church La, Pevensey BN24 40 C3
Church La, Robertsbridge TN32 51 D4
Church La, Rye TN31 38 C6
Church La, St Annes, Lewes BN7 33 E5
Church La, Seaford BN25 49 E5
Church La, South Malling, Lewes BN7 33 F3
Church Pass*, Croft TN34 26 C5
Church Rd, Brighton BN41 43 B4
Church Rd, Crowborough TN6 18 C4
Church Rd, Herstmonceux BN27 29 B3
Church Rd, Lewes BN8 38 D2
Church Rd, Lower Horsebridge BN27 24 B1
Church Rd, Polegate BN26 42 C3
Church Rd, St Leonards TN37 50 C3
Church Rd, Uckfield TN22 31 B5
Church Row BN7 32 A1
Church St TN31 46 C3
Church St, Bexhill TN40 14 D4
Church St, Brighton BN1 16 D3
Church St, Brighton BN41 43 B4
Church St, Eastbourne BN21 20 C2
Church St, Heathfield TN21 28 F4
Church St, Seaford BN25 48 D5
Church St, Uckfield TN22 52 C4
Church St, Ticehurst TN5 51 B3
Church St, Wadhurst TN5 54 F3
Church Twitten BN7 32 B2
Church Vale Rd TN40 14 D3
Church Walk TN22 53 C5
Church Way BN2 17 G2
Churchfield TN35 56 C3
Churchill Cl BN20 20 C2
Churchill Rd, Heathfield TN21 28 C4
Churchill Rd, Lewes BN7 32 D2
Churchill Rd, Seaford BN25 48 C4

Chyngton Av BN25 49 H3
Chyngton Gdns BN25 49 G3
Chyngton La BN25 49 H4
Chyngton Pl BN25 49 G5
Chyngton Rd BN25 49 F5
Chyngton Way BN25 49 G6
Chynington La North BN25 49 H4
Cider Hollow BN27 29 C2
Cinque Foil BN10 39 C1
Cinque Ports St TN31 46 C3
Cinque Ports Way BN25 49 H3
Circus St BN2 17 G3
Cissbury Av BN10 39 E3
Cissbury Cres BN2 45 F4
Civic App TN22 53 C5
Clackhams La TN6 19 H6
Clapham La BN26 12 C5
Clare Rd BN7 32 D3
Claremont TN34 26 A5
Claremont Rd, Bexhill TN39 14 C1
Claremont Rd, Newhaven BN9 36 E4
Claremont Rd, Seaford BN25 48 C4
Claremont Rise TN22 52 D3
Clarence Gdns BN1 16 C4
Clarence Rd, Eastbourne BN22 21 G1
Clarence Rd, St Leonards TN37 50 C2
Clarence Sq BN1 16 C4
Clarence St BN41 43 B5
Clarence Yd BN1 17 E4
Clarendon Pl BN41 43 B5
Clarendon Rd BN3 30 C4
Clarendon Villas BN3 30 C4
Clarke Av BN3 30 A1
Claverham Cl TN33 13 A3
Claverham Way TN33 13 A3
Claxton Rd TN40 15 H3
Clayfields BN10 39 B1
Clement Hill Rd TN34 26 C2
Clement La BN26 42 C4
Clementine Av BN25 48 C3
Cleve Ter BN7 33 E5
Clevedon Rd TN39 14 B2
Cliff Av BN10 39 E4
Cliff Cl BN25 49 E6
Cliff End La TN35 23 F1
Cliff Gdns, Peacehaven BN10 45 H5
Cliff Gdns, Seaford BN25 49 E6
Cliff Park Cl BN10 39 E2
Cliff Rd, Eastbourne BN20 20 D6
Cliff Rd, Seaford BN25 49 E6
Cliff Way TN35 23 E3
Cliffe High St BN7 32 B1
Clifford Ct TN6 18 C4
Clifford Rd TN40 14 D5
Clifton Cl TN34 26 A5
Clifton Hill BN1 16 C1
Clifton Mews BN1 16 C2
Clifton Pl, Brighton BN1 16 C3
Clifton Pl, Rye TN31 46 C3
Clifton Rd, Brighton BN1 16 C2
Clifton Rd, Hastings TN35 27 E1
Clifton Rd, Newhaven BN9 37 D6
Clifton Rise TN40 15 F4
Clifton St BN1 16 D1
Clifton Street Pass BN1 16 D1
Clifton Ter BN1 16 C2
Clifton Way BN10 45 H5
Clinch Green Av TN39 14 A1
Clinton Cres TN38 50 B3
Clinton La BN25 48 D4
Clinton Pl BN25 49 E5
Clinton Way TN35 23 E3
Clive Av TN35 27 E2
Cloisters BN9 37 C6
Close 11 BN23 40 A6
Close 12 BN23 40 A6
Close 6 BN23 40 A6
Close 7 BN23 40 A6
Close 8 BN23 40 A6
Cloudesley Rd TN37 50 C3
Clover Way BN41 43 A1
Cluny St BN7 33 E6
Clyde Pk BN27 25 E6
Clyde Rd TN38 50 C4
Coach House Cotts TN31 34 B5
Coast Rd BN24 41 E4
Coastgaurd Sq BN22 21 H1
Coastguard Cotts TN31 34 A5
Coastguard La TN35 23 A3
Cobald Rd BN24 41 F4
Cobden Pl BN27 25 D6
Cobdown La TN22 34 C3

Cobourg Pl TN34
Cockmount La TN5
Cockshut Rd BN7
Coggins Mill La TN
Coghurst Rd TN35
Colchester Vale RH
Coldharbour Cl TN
Coldharbour Cotts
Culdhorn La BN7
Colebrooke Rd TN3
Coleman Av BN3
Coleman St BN2
Coleridge St BN3
College Grn BN21
College Rd, Bexhill
College Rd, Eastbourne BN21
College Rd, Seaford BN25
Collier Rd, Hastings TN34
Collier Rd, Pevensey BN25
Collington Av TN39
Collington Cl BN20
Collington La East T
Collington Park Cres TN39
Collingwood Av TN2
Collingwood Rise TN
Collinstone Rd TN38
Collinswood Dr TN38
Colonnade Gdns BN
Colonnade Rd BN21
Coltstocks Rd BN20
Combe End TN6
Combermere Rd TN3
Commanders Walk T
Commercial Rd BN2
Common Wood Rise TN6
Comphurst La BN27
Compton Av BN1
Compton Cl TN40
Compton Dr BN20
Compton Place Rd BN20
Compton St BN21
Compton Ter BN27
Conduit Hill TN31
Conifer Cl TN34
Connaught Rd, Eastbourne BN21
Connaught Rd, Hove BN3
Connaught Rd, Seaford BN25
Connaught Ter BN3
Constable Way TN40
Conway Pl BN3
Conway St BN3
Cooden Dr TN39
Cookham Dene TN40
Cookson Gdns TN34
Coombe Cl BN27
Coombe La BN20
Coombe Mdw BN2
Coombe Rd, Eastbourne BN20
Coombe Rd, Lewes BN7
Coombe Rise BN2
Coombe Vale BN2
Cooper Dr TN39
Cooper Ct TN31
Coopers La TN6
Coopers Way BN27
Coopers Wood TN6
Coplands Rise TN31
Coppice Av BN20
Coppice Cl BN20
Coppice Vw TN21
Copwood BN27
Cornelius Av BN9
Cornfield Cl BN25
Cornfield Grn BN27
Cornfield La BN21
Cornfield Rd, Eastbourne BN21
Cornfield Rd, Seaford BN25
Cornfield Ter, Eastbourne BN21
Cornfield Ter, St Leonards TN37
Cornford Cl, Brighton BN41
Cornford Cl, Crowborough TN6
Cornmill Gdns BN27
Cornwall Av BN10
Cornwall Rd TN39
Cornwallis Gdns TN34
Cornwallis St TN34

...er TN34 26 A5
Cotts,
...idge TN32 51 D4
Cotts,
TN5 51 D1
Gdns TN33 13 E3
BN25 49 F6
...I TN34 26 D1
BN9 36 D3
TN35 56 C1
CI BN9 36 A2
Rd,
BN2 44 A2
Rd,
3 30 A1
Rd,
...en BN9 37 B8
N22 52 D1
Rd BN2 44 A2
BN7 32 D2
Ter BN3 30 C6
...Av TN5 14 A3
Dr TN39 14 A3
...se St TN34 26 A5
Rd BN26 42 C4
...ts PI TN6 18 E2
Wood Rd TN5 54 E2
N26 12 B5
Rd BN2 45 F4
Walk TN38 50 A1
St BN3 30 B4
ll Rd BN25 49 G2
...e Av BN20 20 B5
...rne St BN1 16 D4
...ok Rd TN37 50 C2
...wn BN7 32 D6
Rd TN40 14 D5
...n Av BN2 44 C4
...CI TN39 14 B5
Av BN3 30 A2
CI BN7 33 G3
...n Av TN39 14 A5
...CI TN39 14 A4
...n Rise TN39 14 A5
BN9 36 F4
I BN26 42 D1
Rd BN10 39 F3
...eld BN8 38 C1
...eld Rd BN25 48 C5
BN7 32 E2
CI TN5 54 E3
...s La TN31 38 B4
BN26 42 C5
BN25 49 E5
BN25 49 E5
,
...borough TN6 18 D4
...d, Hastings TN34 26 C5
...orks RN77 25 D7
...d TN6 18 D3
...Walk TN34 26 B3
Way BN27 24 C4
...ell Rd BN3 30 D4
...La BN25 49 E5
...a TN5 51 B1
...ane Gdns TN5 51 B2
...t, Hove BN3 16 A3
...st, Polegate BN26 42 C3
,
...onards TN37 50 C4
Way BN7 32 D4
La BN25 49 E5
...field CI BN25 49 E5
...orough Hill TN6 18 D3
...orough Rd BN2 45 E4
...urst La TN39 14 D1
...here Av TN40 14 D3
...here Ter TN40 14 D3
CI,
...ham BN27 25 C6
CI,
...eld TN22 52 D4
...Gdns BN1 16 D3
...Hill BN25 49 E1
...a La TN34 26 B3
Rd BN41 43 A3
...St, Brighton BN1 16 C3
St,
...bourne BN21 20 D1
...ne Ho BN21 20 D2
...eld TN22 20 E1
...eld CI TN40 15 G3
...here Ct BN26 12 B2
...here Path TN22 52 F4
...here Rd,
...vhaven BN9 37 A7
...egate BN26 12 B3
...nere Rd,
...ford BN25 49 G5
...nere Rise TN21 28 C2
...o Dr TN21 28 C3
...erland Gdns TN38 50 B3

Cumberland Rd TN39 14 C1
Cuthbert CI TN39 14 B1
Cypress CI TN38 50 A4
Cyprus PI TN31 46 B3

Dacre Pk BN27 25 F6
Dacre Rd,
  Eastbourne BN20 20 B2
Dacre Rd,
  Hailsham BN27 29 A1
Dacre Rd,
  Newhaven BN9 37 C5
Dairy Grn TN6 19 G6
Dale Rd,
  Forest Row RH18 22 C3
Dale Rd, Lewes BN7 32 D5
Dale Vw Gdns BN3 43 C1
Dale Vw BN3 43 C2
Dalehurst Rd TN39 14 B2
Dales CI BN27 29 D2
Dallington CI TN40 15 H3
Dallington Rd BN3 30 A3
Dalmeny Rd TN39 14 A4
Dalton Rd BN20 20 D5
Damon CI BN10 39 C2
Dana Lodge BN10 45 H6
Dane CI BN25 49 E5
Dane Court CI TN39 14 C3
Dane Rd,
  St Leonards TN38 50 B3
Dane Rd, Seaford BN25 48 D5
Daniel Way TN31 34 B6
Danum CI BN7 24 E3
Daresbury CI TN39 14 B3
Darley Rd BN20 20 C5
Darwall Dr BN25 49 G5
Darwell CI TN32 51 C6
Davenport Pk TN21 28 C2
Daveys La BN7 33 G3
Daveys Ter BN7 33 G4
Davigdor Rd BN3 16 B1
Davis CI TN39 14 B1
De Cham Av TN37 50 D3
De Cham Rd TN37 50 C3
De Grey CI BN7 33 G3
De La Warr Grn BN3 32 D2
De La Warr Mews TN40 14 D5
De La Warr Par TN40 14 D6
De La Warr Rd TN40 15 E4
De Moleyns CI TN40 15 E4
De Montfort Rd BN7 33 E4
De Roos Rd BN21 20 D1
De Walden Mews BN20 20 D5
De Warrenne Rd BN7 33 E4
Deacons Dr BN41 43 B1
Deadmans La TN31 46 C2
Deal Av BN25 49 H2
Dean CI, Portslade-by-Sea
  BN41 43 B1
Doon CI,
  Rottingdean BN2 44 C3
Dean Court Rd BN2 44 B3
Dean Gdns BN41 43 B1
Dean Rd BN25 49 E5
Dean St BN1 16 C3
Deanery CI BN7 33 G2
Deans CI TN39 14 B2
Deans Dr TN39 14 B2
Deans Rd BN26 12 B2
Deepdene TN5 54 F1
Deepdene Gdns TN34 26 D5
Deer Paddock La BN27 25 D6
Delaware Rd BN7 32 D5
Dell CI TN38 50 A1
Delves CI BN8 47 A3
Delves Way BN8 47 B3
Den Hill BN20 20 A1
Dene Path TN22 52 E4
Denham Way TN31 34 B5
Denmark PI TN34 26 B6
Denmark Rd BN41 43 B4
Denmark Ter BN1 16 B2
Denmark Villas BN3 30 C4
Denton CI TN31 46 B2
Denton Dr BN9 36 E3
Denton Rd,
  Eastbourne BN20 20 C5
Denton Rd,
  Newhaven BN9 36 E4
Denton Rise BN9 36 E4
Denton Way BN9 37 C5
Derby PI BN2 17 H4
Derek Av BN3 43 C5
Derwent CI BN27 25 C5
Derwent Rd BN20 20 D5
Devonshire CI BN3 30 D4
Devonshire PI,
  Brighton BN2 17 G5
Devonshire PI,
  Eastbourne BN21 21 F3
Devonshire Rd,
  Bexhill TN40 14 D5
Devonshire Rd,
  Hastings TN34 26 A5

Devonshire Sq TN40 14 D5
Diana CI TN40 15 G2
Dickens Way BN23 40 A6
Dillingham Rd BN20 20 B1
Diplock CI TN38 42 C2
Diplocks Walk BN27 25 C6
Diplocks Way BN27 25 B6
Ditchling Rd BN1 17 G1
Ditchling Way BN27 25 C7
Dittons Rd BN21 20 D3
Dixter La TN31 38 A5
Dixter Rd TN31 38 A5
Dodshill TN6 19 E5
Dogs Hill Rd TN36 55 D4
Donald Way TN36 55 C5
Dordrecht Way TN34 26 A3
Dorothy Av BN10 39 B3
Dorothy Av North BN10 39 C1
Dorothy Rd BN3 43 C3
Dorset Gdns BN2 17 G5
Dorset PI, Brighton BN2 17 G4
Dorset PI,
  Hastings TN34 26 A6
Dorset Rd, Bexhill TN40 15 E5
Dorset Rd, Lewes BN7 33 F5
Dorset Rd South TN40 15 E5
Dorset St BN2 17 G4
Douce Gro TN38 50 A2
Douchs Pass*,
  The Bourne TN34 26 C5
Douglas CI TN37 24 C4
Dove Ct TN22 52 D4
Dover CI BN25 49 H2
Dover Rd BN26 42 D2
Down Rd TN39 14 B3
Downland Av BN10 39 E3
Downland Copse TN22 52 C4
Downland Cres BN3 30 B1
Downlands Av TN39 14 B5
Downlands CI TN39 14 B4
Downline CI TN21 29 B5
Downs CI BN7 32 C3
Downs Rd,
  Hastings TN34 26 A2
Downs Rd,
  Seaford BN25 49 F4
Downs Villas BN9 36 D2
Downside BN7 32 D5
Downside CI BN20 20 B2
Downsvalley Rd BN20 42 C5
Downsview TN21 28 D2
Downsview Cres TN22 52 D4
Downsview Rd,
  Brighton BN41 43 A1
Downsview Rd,
  Eastbourne BN20 42 C5
Downsview Rd,
  Seaford BN25 49 F5
Downsview Way BN27 25 D6
Draffin La TN31 34 A5
Drapers Way TN38 50 B1
Drove Rd BN41 43 A2
Drovers CI BN41 43 B1
Drury La TN38 50 A1
Duchess Dr BN25 49 E1
Dudley Rd,
  Eastbourne BN22 21 G1
Dudley Rd,
  Hastings TN35 26 D3
Duke Mews*,
  Duke St TN37 50 B1
Duke Rd TN37 50 B1
Duke St, Bexhill TN39 14 A4
Duke St, Brighton BN1 16 D4
Duke St,
  St Leonards TN37 50 B1
Duke Ter TN37 50 C1
Dukes CI BN25 48 C3
Dukes Ct BN6 16 D4
Dukes Dr BN20 20 C6
Dukes Hill TN33 13 C2
Dukes La BN1 17 E4
Dulwich CI BN25 49 G3
Dumbrells BN6 35 B4
Dumbrells Court Rd
  BN6 35 B4
Dumbrells Ct BN6 35 B4
Dunbar Dr BN27 25 C5
Dunclutha Rd TN34 26 B1
Dunes Av TN31 34 B6
Dunstan Ter TN5 54 E2
Dunstans Cft TN20 23 D1
Dunvan CI BN7 33 F2
Dursley Rd BN20 21 F2
Dyke Rd BN1 16 C1
Dymchurch CI BN25 49 H3
Dymock CI BN25 49 H3

Eagle CI TN22 53 E7
Earl St TN34 26 B5
Earls CI BN25 48 C3
Earls Gdns BN7 32 A1
East Albany Rd BN25 49 F4

East Ascent TN38 50 B5
East Beach St TN34 26 C5
East Beeches Rd TN6 19 E4
East Bourne St*,
  The Bourne TN34 26 C5
East CI BN26 42 D2
East Dean Rd BN20 20 A4
East Dean Rise BN25 49 G3
East End La BN6 35 B5
East Gdns BN6 35 B5
East Hill Pass TN34 26 D5
East Par TN34 26 C5
East St, Brighton BN1 17 E5
East St, Hastings TN34 26 C5
East St, Lewes BN7 32 B1
East St, Mayfield TN20 23 D1
East St, Portslade-by-Sea
  BN41 43 B5
East St, Rye TN31 46 C3
East St,
  St Leonards TN37 50 C4
East St, Seaford BN25 49 E5
East Way BN7 32 C3
Eastbourne Av BN24 41 F4
Eastbourne Rd,
  Pevensey BN24 40 A5
Eastbourne Rd,
  Pevensey Bay BN24 40 D5
Eastbourne Rd,
  Polegate BN26 42 C3
Eastbourne Rd,
  Seaford BN25 49 G4
Eastbourne Rd,
  Uckfield TN22 53 D7
Eastbourne Ter BN25 49 G4
Eastbridge Rd BN9 37 D6
Eastbrook Rd BN41 43 A4
Eastern Av BN26 42 D2
Eastern Rd BN2 17 H4
Eastgate St BN7 32 B1
Eastgate Wharf BN7 32 B1
Easthill Dr BN41 43 A2
Easthill Way BN41 43 A2
Eastport La BN7 33 F5
Eastwell PI BN27 25 D6
Eastwood Rd TN39 14 B4
Eaton Gdns BN3 30 D4
Eaton Gro BN3 30 D4
Eaton Manor BN3 30 D4
Eaton Rd BN3 30 D5
Eaton Villas BN3 30 C4
Ebenezer Rd TN34 26 D5
Eden Dr TN39 14 A4
Edensor Rd BN20 20 C6
Edgar Rd TN35 27 E3
Edge Hill TN21 28 B2
Edinburgh Rd,
  Bexhill TN40 14 C4
Edinburgh Rd,
  Seaford BN25 48 C4
Edith Av BN10 39 B3
Edith Av North BN10 39 B1
Edith Rd TN35 27 F2
Edmonton Rd TN39 14 C2
Edmund Rd TN35 27 E3
Edward Av BN2 45 E2
Edward CI BN25 48 A1
Edward Rd TN37 50 D4
Edward St,
  Brighton BN2 17 F4
Edward St, Lewes BN7 32 A1
Edwin Rd TN35 27 E3
Effingham CI BN2 45 E3
Egerton Rd TN39 14 B6
Egles Gro TN22 52 B4
Egmont Rd BN3 43 C3
Egremont PI,
  Brighton BN2 17 H4
Egremont PI,
  Hastings TN34 26 D3
Eight Bells CI TN22 31 C5
Eileen Av BN24 44 D4
Elder CI BN41 43 A1
Elderwood CI TN39 14 D1
Eleanor CI, Lewes BN7 33 E3
Eleanor CI,
  Seaford BN25 48 D2
Eleanor Ter TN35 27 F1
Eley Cres BN2 44 A2
Eley Dr BN2 44 A1
Elgin Gdns BN25 49 H4
Elim Court Gdns TN6 18 C2
Elizabeth Av BN3 30 B1
Elizabeth CI BN25 48 A1
Elizabeth Ct BN27 25 E6
Elizabeth Rd TN38 50 A1
Ellen St, Brighton BN41 43 A1
Ellen St, Hove BN3 30 C4
Ellenslea Rd TN37 50 C4
Elleslie La TN39 14 A2
Elliots Way TN21 28 C1
Ellis CI TN34 26 A5
Ellis Way TN22 53 B5
Ellison CI TN6 18 C2

Elm CI BN25 49 H4
Elm Ct BN9 37 B6
Elm Dr, Hove BN3 30 A3
Elm Dr, Portslade-by-Sea
  BN3 43 D2
Elm Grn BN27 24 D4
Elm Gro BN7 32 A2
Elm Rd BN41 43 A3
Elm Way TN21 28 D3
Elmhurst Gdns BN27 29 A1
Elmore Rd BN2 17 H3
Elms Av BN21 21 G3
Elms Rd BN21 21 G3
Elmsdown PI BN27 25 E6
Elmstead Rd TN40 15 E3
Elphick PI TN6 18 D3
Elphick Rd, Lewes BN8 47 C2
Elphick Rd,
  Newhaven BN9 37 C5
Elphinstone Av TN34 26 B2
Elphinstone Gdns TN34 26 B2
Elphinstone Rd TN34 26 B1
Elrington Rd BN3 30 D2
Elven Cres BN2 44 A1
Ely Ct BN7 32 B1
Emmanuel Rd TN34 26 C4
Endwell Rd TN40 14 D5
English CI BN3 30 A3
Englishs Pass BN7 32 C1
Enys Rd BN21 21 E2
Epsom CI TN38 50 B3
Eridge CI TN39 14 A5
Eridge Dr TN6 19 E3
Eridge Gdns TN6 19 E3
Eridge Grn BN7 33 E3
Eridge Rd,
  Crowborough TN6 18 D3
Eridge Rd, Hove BN3 30 B1
Erroll Rd BN3 43 C5
Ersham Rd BN27 25 D8
Ersham Way BN27 25 D7
Esher CI BN7 49 F3
Esplanade,
  Brighton BN1 16 A4
Esplanade,
  Seaford BN25 48 D5
Esplanade Mews BN25 49 E5
Essenden Rd TN38 50 A5
Essex Mews BN9 37 C5
Essex PI BN9 37 C5
Essex St BN2 17 H5
Estate Rd BN9 37 D5
Ethel St BN3 30 C4
Etherton Way BN25 49 F3
Eton CI BN25 49 F3
Eton Mews BN21 21 F2
Evelyn Av BN9 37 B5
Evelyn Rd BN7 33 E3
Evorofield CI TN37 50 D5
Eversfield Rd BN21 21 E1
Eversley CI TN37 50 C1
Eversley Cres TN37 50 C1
Eversley Rd,
  Bexhill TN40 14 D6
Eversley Rd,
  St Leonards TN37 50 C1
Ewart St BN2 17 H1
Ewhurst CI TN34 26 A1
Ewhurst La TN31 38 A6
Exmouth PI TN34 26 C5

Factory La BN27 25 C7
Fair La TN32 51 C,D5
Fair Mdw TN31 46 C2
Faircrouch La TN5 54 A1
Fairfield,
  Hailsham BN27 29 A1
Fairfield,
  Peacehaven BN10 39 B2
Fairfield Chase TN39 14 A4
Fairfield Gdns BN41 43 B2
Fairfield Rd BN20 20 D4
Fairglen Cotts TN5 54 A4
Fairglen Rd TN5 54 A4
Fairholme Rd BN9 36 E4
Fairhurst BN10 45 H6
Fairisle CI BN27 24 C4
Fairlawns Dr BN27 29 A1
Fairlight TN22 52 E3
Fairlight Av,
  Hastings TN35 27 F1
Fairlight Av,
  Peacehaven BN10 39 B2
Fairlight CI, Bexhill TN40 15 H3
Fairlight CI,
  Polegate BN26 42 D3
Fairlight Fld BN8 47 B3
Fairlight Gdns TN35 23 D3
Fairlight Rd,
  Fairlight TN35 23 A3
Fairlight Rd,
  Hastings TN35 27 F1
Fairmount Rd TN40 15 E4
Fairoak CI TN21 28 C2

Fairstone Cl TN35 27 F1
Fairview Cotts TN6 18 C2
Fairview La TN6 18 C2
Fairway Cl BN20 20 B3
Fairway Cres BN41 43 B1
Fairways Cl BN25 49 H5
Fairways Rd BN25 49 G5
Falaise Rd,
  Newhaven BN9 36 F4
Falaise Rd,
  St Leonards TN37 50 D4
Falcon Way BN27 24 D3
Falconers Dr TN33 13 E3
Fallowfield Cl BN3 30 A1
Fallowfield Cres BN3 30 A1
Falmer Av BN2 44 D2
Falmer Ct TN22 52 D4
Falmer Rd BN2 44 A1
Farley Bank TN34 26 D3
Farley Way TN35 23 C3
Farm Cl, Brighton BN41 43 A1
Farm Cl, Seaford BN25 49 G3
Farm La, Hassocks BN6 35 C5
Farm La, Rye TN31 34 A5
Farm Yd BN1 16 D4
Farman St BN3 16 A3
Farmland Way BN27 24 E4
Farmlands Cl BN26 42 C5
Farmlands Cl BN26 42 C5
Farmlands Way BN26 42 B4
Farmway Cl BN3 43 C1
Farncombe Rd BN7 32 C1
Farne Cl BN27 24 B4
Farningham Rd TN6 19 G6
Farriers Pl BN8 47 B3
Farriers Way TN22 53 C6
Farthing Hill TN5 51 C2
Faygate Cl TN39 14 C1
Fayre Mdw TN32 51 D5
Fazan Ct TN5 54 E4
Fearon Rd TN34 26 A3
Fellows Rd TN34 26 C2
Fermor Row TN6 18 D6
Fermor Way TN6 18 D6
Fern Grn BN27 24 D4
Fern Rd TN38 50 A2
Fernlea Cl TN35 56 C1
Ferrers Rd BN7 32 D3
Ferring Cl TN31 46 B3
Ferry Hill TN36 55 A2
Ferry Rd TN31 46 B2
Festival Gdns TN39 14 D1
Field Cl BN25 49 H5
Field End TN22 34 A3
Field Vw TN22 51 C6
Fielden La TN6 18 B6
Fielden Rd TN6 18 B3
Fieldway BN6 35 B5
Fiennes Rd BN27 29 A1
Figg La TN6 18 D6
Filching Cl TN6 42 B6
Filsham Dr TN40 15 H2
Filsham Rd TN38 50 A4
Filsham Valley TN38 50 A4
Findon Av BN2 45 F4
Findon Cl BN25 49 H5
Finsbury Rd BN2 17 H2
Fir Toll Cl TN20 23 A2
Fir Toll Rd TN20 23 A2
Fir Tree Cl BN27 24 E4
Firehills Cotts TN35 23 A4
Firle Cl, Hastings TN35 27 F1
Firle Cl, Seaford BN25 48 D3
Firle Cres BN7 32 C3
Firle Dr BN25 49 E2
Firle Grange BN25 49 E2
Firle Grn TN22 52 E3
Firle Rd,
  Eastbourne BN22 21 G1
Firle Rd,
  Peacehaven BN10 39 B1
Firle Rd, Seaford BN25 49 E2
Firle Ter BN9 36 D3
First Av, Bexhill TN40 15 G3
First Av, Hove BN3 30 D6
First Av, Newhaven BN9 37 C6
First Av, Rye TN31 34 B6
Firtree Rd TN34 26 C2
Firwood Cl TN21 28 C1
Firwood Rise TN21 28 C1
Fisher St BN7 32 A1
Fishergate Cl BN41 43 A4
Fishergate Ter BN41 43 A4
Fishmarket Rd TN31 46 C1
Fishponds La TN35 56 D3
Fitzgerald Av BN25 49 F5
Fitzgerald Cl BN20 21 E5
Fitzgerald Pk BN25 49 F5
Fitzgerald Rd BN7 33 G2
Fitzjohns Rd BN7 32 D3
Fitzroy Rd BN7 32 D2
Five Villages Ho TN36 31 C2
Fleetway Cl TN31 34 B5
Fletcher Cl BN27 25 E7

Fletching St TN20 23 C2
Flint Cl, Brighton BN41 43 B1
Flint Cl, Seaford BN25 48 D1
Florence Av BN3 43 C3
Folkestone Cl BN41 49 H2
Folkington Rd BN26 42 A3
Fonthill Rd BN3 30 C3
Foords La TN21 29 D4
Ford Rd TN38 50 A1
Foredown Cl,
  Brighton BN41 43 B1
Foredown Cl,
  Eastbourne BN20 20 B3
Foredown Dr BN41 43 B2
Foredown Rd BN41 43 A1
Forest Dene TN6 19 G5
Forest Lodge TN6 18 B6
Forest Pk,
  Crowborough TN6 18 B4
Forest Pk, Uckfield TN22 34 A3
Forest Rd RH18 22 B3
Forest Rise TN6 19 G5
Forest Vw BN27 25 C5
Forest Way TN34 26 A4
Forge Cl, Brighton BN41 43 B1
Forge Cl, Uckfield TN22 53 C6
Forge Rise TN22 53 C6
Fort Rd BN9 37 D6
Fort Rise BN9 37 D7
Forward Cl BN9 36 D3
Foster Cl BN25 49 E3
Foundry La BN7 32 C1
Foundry St BN1 17 E3
Founthill Av BN2 44 D4
Founthill Rd BN2 44 D3
Fourth Av BN3 30 C6
Fox Way BN41 43 A1
Foxglove Cl BN8 47 D1
Foyle Way BN20 20 D6
Framfield Rd,
  Buxted TN22 31 B5
Framfield Rd,
  Uckfield TN22 53 D6
Franklin Rd BN41 43 B4
Frant Rd BN3 30 B1
Frederick Gdns BN1 17 E3
Frederick Pl BN1 17 E2
Frederick Rd TN35 26 D1
Frederick St BN1 17 E3
Freeland Cl BN25 48 A1
Freemans Rd BN41 43 A3
Frenches Farm Dr TN21 28 C4
Freshfield Bank RH18 22 B3
Freshfield Dr BN27 25 D7
Freshwater Av TN34 26 A2
Freshwater Sq BN22 42 D6
Frewen Cl TN31 38 B5
Friars Av BN10 39 D3
Friars Rd TN36 55 B3
Friars Walk BN7 32 B2
Friars Way TN34 26 B1
Friston Cl BN25 48 C3
Frith Rd BN3 30 B3
Front Cotts TN5 51 C2
Fryatts Way TN39 14 A3
Fulford Cl TN38 50 A3
Fuller Cl TN5 54 D3
Fuller Rd BN7 32 D2
Fullers La TN31 38 C6
Fullers Pass BN7 32 B1
Fullwood Av BN9 37 B5
Furnace Way TN22 53 E5
Furness Rd BN20 21 E3
Furze Cft BN3 16 A2
Furze Hill BN3 16 A2
Furze Hill Ct BN3 16 A2
Fyrsway TN35 23 C4

Gage Ridge RH18 22 B3
Gainsborough La BN26 42 B3
Gainsborough Rd TN40 15 F3
Galley Hill Vw TN40 15 F5
Garden Cl, Bexhill TN40 14 D5
Garden Cl,
  Brighton BN41 43 B3
Garden Mews BN20 20 C5
Garden St BN7 32 A2
Gardener St BN41 43 A3
Gardeners Hill BN9 36 F3
Gardner Rd BN41 43 A4
Gardner St,
  Brighton BN1 17 E3
Gardner St,
  Hailsham BN27 29 B1
Gardner Way TN38 50 B5
Garfield Rd BN27 25 D6
Garth Cl TN39 14 B3
Gatelands Dr TN39 14 B3
Gaudick Cl BN20 20 D5
Gaudick Rd BN20 20 D4
Gavin Astor Cl TN40 15 G3
Geary Pl TN35 56 C2
Geering Rd BN27 25 F6
Geers Wood TN21 28 B3

Geneva Rd BN9 37 C7
Gensing Rd TN38 50 C4
George Hill TN32 51 C6
George Mews TN33 13 C3
George St,
  Brighton BN2 17 G5
George St,
  Hailsham BN27 25 D6
George St,
  Hastings TN34 26 C5
George St, Hove BN3 30 C5
George St, Portslade-by-Sea BN41 43 B5
George St,
  Wadhurst TN5 54 E2
Georgian Cl TN40 15 E3
Gerald Rd BN25 49 F6
German St TN36 55 A2
Ghyll Rd,
  Crowborough TN6 18 B2
Ghyll Rd,
  Heathfield TN21 28 B2
Ghyllside Rd TN31 38 B4
Gibb Cl TN40 15 G3
Gibbon Rd BN9 37 B6
Gibraltar Rise TN21 28 C2
Gilbert Rd,
  Eastbourne BN22 21 G1
Gilbert Rd,
  St Leonards TN38 50 B3
Gilbert Way BN27 25 D8
Gilda Cres BN26 42 C3
Gildredge Rd,
  Eastbourne BN21 21 F3
Gildredge Rd,
  Seaford BN25 49 E4
Gilham La RH18 22 B2
Gillridge Grn TN6 18 D2
Gillsmans Dr TN38 50 A2
Gillsmans Hill TN38 50 A2
Githa Rd TN35 27 E3
Gladstone Rd,
  Brighton BN41 43 A4
Gladstone Rd,
  Crowborough TN6 18 D5
Gladstone Ter TN34 26 C4
Gladys Av BN10 39 D3
Gladys Rd BN3 43 C3
Glassenbury Dr TN40 15 G4
Glastonbury Rd BN3 43 C5
Glebe Cl,
  Eastbourne BN20 20 C2
Glebe Cl, Lewes BN7 32 D5
Glebe Dr BN25 49 E4
Glebe Villas BN3 43 C4
Glen Cl BN26 42 B5
Glenburn TN39 14 D1
Glendor Rd BN3 43 D5
Gleneagles Cl,
  Bexhill TN40 15 F4
Gleneagles Cl,
  Seaford BN25 48 A1
Gleneagles Dr BN27 24 B4
Glengorse TN33 13 E4
Glengorse Ct TN33 13 E4
Glenleigh Av TN39 14 A2
Glenleigh Park Rd TN39 14 A2
Glenleigh Walk TN32 51 B5
Glenmore Mews BN21 21 F2
Glenmore Rd TN6 18 A3
Glenmore Rd East TN6 18 B3
Glenthorn Rd TN39 14 B4
Glenview Ct TN35 27 E3
Gleton Av BN3 43 D1
Gloucester Av TN40 15 H4
Gloucester Pass BN1 17 F2
Gloucester Pl BN1 17 F3
Gloucester Rd,
  Brighton BN1 17 E2
Gloucester Rd,
  Wadhurst TN5 54 E2
Gloucester St BN1 17 F2
Glovers La TN39 14 D2
Glyn Cl BN10 39 B3
Glynde Av BN2 45 E3
Glynde Cl BN9 36 D3
Glyndebourne Av BN2 45 E3
Glyne Ascent TN40 15 F4
Glyne Barn Cl TN40 15 H3
Glyne Dr TN40 15 G3
Goddens Cl TN31 38 C4
Goddens Ghyll TN31 38 B5
Godfrey Cl BN7 33 F2
Godwin Rd,
  Hastings TN35 26 D3
Godwin Rd, Hove BN3 43 C3
Goldbridge Rd BN8 38 D1
Goldcrest Dr TN40 15 D7
Golden La BN1 16 A4
Golden Miller La BN26 42 B3
Goldhurst Grn TN36 31 C2
Goldsmith Av TN6 18 C3
Goldsmith Cl BN23 40 A6
Goldstone Cl BN3 30 C1

Goldstone Cres BN3 30 B1
Goldstone La BN3 30 C3
Goldstone Rd BN3 30 C4
Goldstone St BN3 30 C4
Goldstone Villas BN3 30 C4
Goodwin Cl BN27 24 B4
Goodwood Cl TN40 14 D2
Gordon P1 TN39 14 C3
Gordon Rd,
  Crowborough TN6 18 D4
Gordon Rd, Portslade-by-Sea,
  Portslade-by-Sea BN41 43 A4
Gordon Rd,
  Hailsham BN27 25 D7
Gordon Rd,
  Hastings TN34 26 C4
Gordon Rd, Portslade-by-Sea
  BN41 43 B4
Gordon Rd,
  Uckfield TN22 31 B5
Gore Park Av BN21 20 C1
Gore Park Rd BN21 20 C1
Gorham Av BN2 44 C3
Gorham Cl BN2 44 C3
Gorham Way BN10 45 G5
Gorringe Cl BN20 42 D6
Gorringe Dr BN20 42 D6
Gorringe Rd BN21 21 F1
Gorringe Valley Rd
  BN20 42 C6
Gorse Dr BN25 49 F1
Gorsethorn Way TN35 23 D4
Gosford Way BN26 42 C3
Gote La BN8 47 A5
Grafton St BN2 17 H6
Grand Av, Bexhill TN40 15 G3
Grand Av, Hove BN3 30 D6
Grand Av,
  Seaford BN25 48 C2
Grand Cres BN2 44 C3
Grand Junction Rd BN1 17 E5
Grand Par, Brighton BN2 17 F4
Grand Par,
  Eastbourne BN21 21 F4
Grand Par,
  Polegate BN26 42 B3
Grand Par,
  St Leonards TN37,38 50 C5
Grand Par Mews BN2 17 F4
Grange Cl,
  Crowborough TN6 18 B5
Grange Cl,
  Heathfield TN21 29 A6
Grange Court Dr TN39 14 C3
Grange Cl,
  Eastbourne BN22 21 E3
Grange Ct, Lewes BN7 33 E5
Grange Gdns BN22 21 E3
Grange Rd,
  Eastbourne BN22 21 E3
Grange Rd, Hove BN3 30 A4
Grange Rd, Lewes BN7 33 E5
Grange Rd,
  Uckfield TN22 53 D5
Grant St BN2 17 H1
Granville Ct BN20 21 E4
Granville Rd BN22 21 E3
Grassington Rd BN22 21 E3
Grassmere Av BN10 45 H5
Gray Ct TN21 28 B2
Graycoats Dr TN35 18 D4
Graystone La TN35 27 E2
Great Rough BN8 38 A2
Greater Paddock BN8 47 C3
Green Cl BN8 47 B2
Green Gro BN27 25 D6
Green La,
  Crowborough TN6 19 F4
Green La,
  Heathfield TN21 28 D3
Green La, Lowoe BN7 32 A2
Green La, Seaford BN25 48 D5
Green Sq,
  Brighton BN2 44 B3
Green Sq,
  Wadhurst TN5 54 E3
Green St TN36 20 B1
Green Walk,
  Hailsham BN27 24 E4
Green Walk,
  Seaford BN25 49 G5
Green Wall BN7 32 B1
Greenacres,
  Hastings TN35 56 C3
Greenacres,
  Peacehaven BN10 45 H6
Greenacres Dr,
  Hailsham BN27 25 E6
Greenacres Dr,
  Lewes BN8 47 A4
Greenacres Way BN27 25 E6
Greenbank Av BN3 43 C4
Greenfield Dr TN22 53 D8
Greenfield Rd BN21 20 C2

Greenfields BN27
Greenleaf Gdns BN.
Greenleas BN3
Greenways,
  Bexhill TN39
Greenways,
  Brighton BN2
Greenwell Cl BN25
Greenwich Rd BN27
Greenwich Way BN1
Gregory La BN24
Grennan Ct TN35
Grenville Rd BN24
Grenville St BN1
Gresham Way TN38
Greville Rd TN35
Greville Ct BN7
Greyfriars Pl TN36
Greys Rd BN20
Grosvenor Cl BN26
Grosvenor Rd BN25
Grosvenor St BN2
Grove Bank BN2
Grove Hill BN2
Grove Rd,
  Eastbourne BN21
Grove Rd,
  Hastings TN35
Grove Rd,
  Seaford BN25
Grove St BN2
Grovelands Rd BN27
Growers End BN8
Guardian Ct BN26
Guardswell Pl BN25
Guildford Rd BN1
Guildford St BN1
Guinness Trust Bungal
  BN9
Guldeford Rd TN31
Gundreda Rd BN7
Gunters La TN39
Gurth Rd TN35
Gwyneth Gro TN40

Haddington Cl BN3
Haddington St BN3
Hailsham Av BN2
Hailsham By-Pass BN2:
Hailsham Rd,
  Hailsham BN27
Hailsham Rd,
  Heathfield TN21
Hailsham Rd,
  Herstmonceux BN27
Hailsham Rd,
  Horam TN21
Hailsham Rd,
  Polegate BN26
Halley Pk BN27
Halley Rd TN21
Halls Cotts TN5
Hallyburton Rd BN3
Halton Cres TN34
Halton Rd BN22
Halton Ter TN34
Ham La, Lewes BN7
Ham La, Ringmer BN8
Hamelsham Ct BN27
Hamilton Gdns TN35
Hamilton Ter TN39
Hamlands La BN22
Hampden Cl TN33
Hampden Gdns BN9
Hampden Ter BN22
Hampton Ho BN27
Hampton Pl BN1
Hampton St BN1
Hamsey Cres BN7
Hamsey La BN25
Hamsey Rd BN22
Hangleton Cl BN3
Hangleton Gdns BN3
Hangleton La BN3,41
Hangleton Link Rd BN41
Hangleton Manor Cl
  BN3
Hangleton Rd BN3
Hangleton Valley Dr
  BN3
Hangleton Way BN3
Hanover Cl,
  Bexhill TN40
Hanover Cl,
  Seaford BN25
Hanover Ct BN27
Hanover Rd BN22
Hanover St BN2
Hanover Ter BN2
Hanson Rd BN9
Harbour Barn TN36
Harbour Rd TN31
Harbour View Cl BN25

60

ew Rd BN9 37 A7
TN22 53 D6
d TN22 53 D6
d BN21 37 E3
Rd TN34 26 D3
g CI BN27 24 E3
g Cres BN27 24 E3
g Dr BN27 24 D3
g Gdns BN27 24 E3
g La BN27 24 E4
e Rd TN6 18 C6
e Rise TN6 18 D6
CI TN39 14 A5
BN9 34 E3
d BN25 49 G4
Mews TN22 53 E7
La TN6 18 C5
PI TN6 18 C6
TN21 28 C3
Hay Rd BN27 24 D4
Hill BN8 38 B1
BN24 41 G2
ews TN38 50 C5
TN34 26 B5
TN34,35 26 D4
r TN33 13 E4
Rd BN9 37 C5
s TN33 13 F3
s La BN8 47 B4
CI BN25 49 F3
N22 53 B5
La BN21 21 E1
Rd,
n BN2 45 F4
Rd,
urne BN21 21 E2
Rd,
Row RH18 22 C2
Rd,
d BN25 49 F4
Combe TN38 50 B3
on PI BN21 21 F3
on Villas BN3 30 C3
d Lodge TN40 14 D5
CI BN7 33 F2
Rd BN8 47 A4
Way BN7 32 C1
Cres TN40 15 G3
Av BN25 49 H2
Rd,
N33 13 F4
Rd,
TN40 15 E4
d RH18 22 C3
r Rd TN37 50 C4
r Rd,
TN40 14 D3
r Rd,
urne BN22 21 G1
k Rd,
gs TN34 26 A5
Brow BN25 49 F3
CI BN24 41 G3
bury Way BN7 32 D4
s Way BN27 25 D6
Farm CI BN27 24 D3
Rd BN27 24 C4
own CI BN27 24 D3
own Cres BN27 24 D3
own Gdns BN27 24 D3
own Vw BN27 24 D3
wood Dr BN27 24 E3
wood Rd BN27 24 D3
CI BN25 48 B3
Cres BN25 48 B3
Gro BN25 48 C3
Hill BN25 48 B3
Park Rd BN25 48 B3
PI BN25 48 C3
Rise BN25 48 B3
Way BN25 48 C4
orn CI BN2 45 E3
orn Rd TN35 27 F2
orn Rise BN9 37 B6
orne CI TN21 28 D3
ylands Cres
7 24 D4
ylands Dr BN27 24 D4
ylands Rd BN27 24 D4
CI,
hton BN41 43 B3
CI, Lewes BN8 47 A4
Plat TN31 38 C6
nd Grn BN27 24 E4
ard Rd BN7 32 D2
CI BN9 37 B6
Gro BN20 42 C6
dene BN25 49 G5
wood Cotts TN5 51 B2
land Av BN25 49 F5
land CI BN10 39 E2
ner Walk TN6 19 G5
ner Way TN35 23 D4
herdune Rd TN39 14 B3

Heathfield Av BN9 45 E2
Heathfield Gdns TN32 51 C6
Heathfield Rd BN25 49 F5
Heathlands TN35 56 C3
Heavegate Rd TN35 18 A5
Heighton Cres BN9 36 D3
Heighton Rd BN9 36 D2
Helena CI BN41 43 B2
Helensdene Walk TN37 50 C3
Hempstead Gdns TN22 53 D5
Hempstead La,
Hailsham BN27 25 A6
Hempstead La,
Uckfield TN22 52 F4
Hempstead La,
Uckfield TN22 53 D5
Hempstead Rd,
Brighton BN2 45 F2
Hempstead Rd,
Uckfield TN22 53 D5
Hempstead Rise TN22 53 D5
Henderson CI TN34 26 A2
Henge Way BN41 43 A1
Henley CI TN31 46 A3
Henry Ter*,
All Saints St TN34 26 D5
Hereford St BN2 17 H5
Hereward Way BN7 33 G3
Herne Rd TN6 18 D6
Heron CI TN22 53 D7
Heron Ridge BN26 42 D3
Hever Cres TN39 14 A3
Higglers CI TN22 31 B6
Higgs Ct BN27 25 C5
High Bank TN35 27 E2
High Bank TN35 27 F2
High CI BN41 43 A2
High Cross Flds TN6 18 D3
High Fords TN36 31 C2
High Fords CI TN36 31 C2
High Hurst CI BN8 38 C2
High Mdw TN31 38 B5
High Park CI TN31 38 A5
High St, Alfriston BN26 12 B3
High St, Battle TN33 13 C3
High St, Bexhill TN40 14 D4
High St, Brighton BN2 17 G5
High St, Buxted TN22 31 A5
High St, Camber TN22 34 B3
High St,
Crowborough TN6 18 D3
High St,
Eastbourne BN21 20 D2
High St, Hailsham BN27 25 D5
High St, Hassocks BN6 35 B5
High St, Hastings TN34 26 C5
High St, Heathfield TN21 28 A2
High St, Lewes BN7 33 E5
High St, Mayfield TN20 23 B1
High St, Newhaven BN8 38 C1
High St, Pevensey BN24 40 C3
High St, Polegate BN26 42 C3
High St, Portslade-by-Sea
BN41 43 A2
High St,
Robertsbridge TN32 51 C5
High St,
Rottingdean BN2 44 B4
High St, Rye TN31 46 C3
High St, Seaford BN25 49 E5
High St, Ticehurst TN5 51 A2
High St, Uckfield TN22 53 D5
High St, Wadhurst TN5 54 A3
High St, Westham TN24 40 R3
High St,
Winchelsea TN36 55 A2
High View Ct BN20 20 D3
High Wickham TN34 26 D4
Higham Grn TN36 55 A2
Higham La TN31 38 A5
Highcroft Cres TN21 28 C2
Highdown Rd BN7 32 C3
Highfield Gdns TN39 14 D2
Highfield Rd TN21 29 B5
Highfields RH18 22 C2
Highgate Rd RH18 22 C4
Highgrove TN33 13 A3
Highlands Av TN22 53 D7
Highlands CI,
Bexhill TN39 14 A1
Highlands CI,
Crowborough TN6 18 C3
Highlands Dr TN38 50 B4
Highlands Gdns TN38 50 B4
Highlands Rd,
Brighton BN41 43 B3
Highlands Rd,
Seaford BN25 49 E4
Highview CI TN22 53 D8
Highview La TN22 53 D8
Highview Rd BN10 45 G5
Highways BN41 43 A1
Hilary CI BN26 42 B4

Hilders Cliff TN31 46 C3
Hilders Farm CI TN6 19 F5
Hilders Farm Ct TN6 19 F5
Hill CI TN6 18 C5
Hill Crest Rd BN9 37 B7
Hill Rd, Brighton BN2 44 D4
Hill Rd, Hastings TN35 23 A3
Hill Rd, Lewes BN7 32 D3
Hill Rd, Newhaven BN9 36 E3
Hill Rd,
Peacehaven BN10 39 F3
Hill Rise,
Newhaven BN9 36 E3
Hill Rise, Seaford BN25 48 B2
Hill Side BN9 37 C6
Hill St TN34 26 C5
Hilbury Gdns TN5 51 B2
Hillcrest TN31 46 C1
Hillcrest Av TN39 14 B2
Hillfield BN7 32 D5
Hillgrove Rd BN2 45 E2
Hillman CI BN7 32 C2
Hillrise TN6 19 F4
Hillside, Brighton BN41 43 B2
Hillside,
Forest Row RH18 22 C2
Hillside Av BN25 49 H2
Hillside Dr TN31 29 A5
Hillside Rd, Bexhill TN40 14 C4
Hillside Rd,
Hastings TN34 26 A1
Hilltop Dr TN31 46 C1
Hillyfield, Lewes BN7 33 E5
Hillyfield, Rye TN31 46 C2
Hillyglen CI TN34 50 D3
Hindover Cres BN25 49 F4
Hindover Rd BN25 49 F4
Hoad Rd BN22 21 G1
Hoadleys La TN6 18 B1
Hoads Wood Rd TN34 26 B1
Hoathdown Av BN9 37 A5
Hobney Rise BN24 40 B4
Hoddern Av BN10 39 A2
Hogarth Rd BN3 30 A5
Hogtrough La TN36 55 A3
Holbrook CI BN26 21 E5
Hole Farm CI TN34 26 A2
Hollamby Pk BN27 25 F7
Holland St BN2 17 H2
Holliers Hill TN40 14 D2
Hollington Ct TN38 50 A3
Hollington Park CI TN38 50 A2
Hollington Park Rd TN38 50 A2
Holly CI,
Hailsham BN27 25 D8
Holly CI,
Heathfield TN21 28 C3
Holly Ct TN6 18 B4
Holly Dr TN21 28 C3
Hollybank Gdns TN38 50 B2
Hollydene Rd TN5 54 E1
Holmdale Rd BN9 36 F4
Holmes Av BN3 30 A2
Holmes CI BN25 48 A1
Holmesdale Gdns TN34 26 A5
Holmesdale Rd TN6 14 B5
Holmsdale CI TN5 54 D2
Holters Way BN25 49 E2
Holyhead CI BN27 25 B5
Holywell CI BN20 20 D6
Holywell CI BN20 20 D6
Holywell Walk BN27 25 D7
Homebush Av BN2 45 F4
Homefield CI BN25 49 E3
Homefield Rd BN25 49 C3
Homelands CI TN39 14 B2
Honeycrag CI BN26 42 C2
Honeysuckle Dr BN27 25 D8
Honeyway CI BN26 42 B6
Honies Ct TN39 14 C3
Hookswood CI TN6 19 E3
Hoopers CI BN7 33 F2
Hopfield Gdns TN22 53 E5
Hopgarden CI TN34 50 D3
Horam Park CI TN21 29 B6
Horebeech La TN21 29 A6
Horntye Rd TN37 50 C2
Horsegrove Av TN5 51 D2
Horseshoe CI TN38 50 B1
Horsfield Rd BN7 33 E2
Horsham Av North
BN10 39 B1
Houndean CI BN7 32 C5
Houndean Rise BN7 32 C5
Hova Villas BN3 30 C5
Hove Park Gdns BN3 30 C3
Hove Park CI BN3 30 C2
Hove Park Villas BN3 30 C3
Hove Park Way BN3 30 D2
Hove PI BN3 30 C6
Hove Seaside Villas
BN41 43 C6
Hove St BN3 30 B5
Hove St South BN3 30 B6

Howard CI BN27 25 F7
Howard Sq BN21 21 F4
Howbourne La TN22 31 D4
Howey CI BN9 36 F4
Howlett Dr BN27 24 D3
Hoyle Rd BN10 39 C2
Huggetts La BN22 42 D6
Hughenden PI TN34 26 B3
Hughenden Rd TN34 26 B3
Hughes Way TN22 52 D4
Hunters Way TN22 52 D4
Hunting CI TN40 14 D4
Huntingdon Rd TN6 18 D6
Hurdis Rd BN25 48 A1
Hurrell Rd TN34 26 D2
Hurst Cres BN41 43 A3
Hurst La,
Eastbourne BN21 20 D1
Hurst La,
Hailsham BN27 29 D2
Hurst Rd BN21 20 C1
Hurstwood CI TN40 15 H3
Hurtis Hill TN6 18 D6
Hyde Gdns TN21 21 F3
Hyde Rd BN21 21 E3
Hyde Tynings CI BN20 20 C5
Hydehurst CI TN6 18 D5
Hylands Yard*,
The Mint TN31 46 C3
Hyperion Av BN26 42 A3
Hythe CI BN25 49 H3
Hythe Cres BN25 49 H3
Hythe Vw BN25 49 H3

Ian CI TN40 15 G2
Idens La TN21 28 F1
Ifield CI BN24 45 G3
Iford CI BN9 36 D3
Ilex Grn BN27 24 D4
Imperial Arc BN1 16 D4

INDUSTRIAL & RETAIL:
Arndale Centre BN21 21 F2
Avis Way BN9 36 D4
Bellbrook Ind Est TN22 53 B6
Brightwell Ind Est BN9 37 D5
Bross Est BN9 37 D5
Burfield Pk Ind Est
BN27 25 C7
Churchill Sq Shopping
Centre BN1 16 D4
Clarks Ind Est BN3 30 C3
Cliffe Ind Est BN7 33 H5
Cradle Hill Ind Est
BN25 49 G2
Delanair Ind Est BN7 33 G3
Durgates Ind Est TN5 54 D2
Euro Bsns Pk BN9 36 D4
Fernbank Centre TN6 18 C3
Euro Bsns Pk
RH18 22 D2
Goldstone Retail Pk
BN3 30 C3
Hailsham Ind Pk BN27 25 C6
Hove Enterprise Centre
BN41 43 C5
Leap Cross Small Bsns
Centre BN27 24 C4
Lewes Bsns Centre
BN7 33 F3
Lexden Lodge Ind Est
TN6 19 G6
Little Sherwood Ind Pk
TN36 31 B2
Malling Brook Ind Est
BN7 33 G3
Meridian Centre BN10 39 B1
Meridian Ind Est BN10 39 C2
Millbrook Bsns Pk TN6 19 H6
Millbrook Ind Est TN6 19 H6
Mountney Bri Bsns Pk
BN24 40 B5
Paradise Pk BN9 36 D4
Phoenix Ind Est BN7 33 F4
Ponswood Ind Est
TN38 50 B1
Portland Rd Ind Est
BN3 43 C3
Potts Marsh Ind Est
BN24 40 A5
Priory Mdw Shopping Centre
TN34 26 B5
Ravenside Retail
& Leisure Pk TN40 15 G4
Ridgewood Park (Ind Pk)
TN22 53 E8
Ringmer Bsns Centre
BN8 47 D3
Riverside Ind Est BN7 33 F3
Rye Ind Est TN31 46 D3
Sackville Ind Est BN3 30 C3
St Joseph Bsns Pk
BN3 30 B3

Southdowns Bsns Pk
BN7 33 G3
Station Rd Ind Est
BN27 25 E8
Sussex Ho Bsns Pk
BN3 30 A3
Suttons Ind Pk TN36 55 C2
Swan Barn Bsns Centre
BN27 25 F8
The Knoll Bsns Centre
BN3 43 C3
Wadhurst Bsns Pk TN5 54 A1
Wealdon Ind Est TN6 19 F6
Wheel Farm Bsns Pk
TN35
Willow Ind Est BN9 36 E4
Ingleside Dr TN6 18 C4
Ingram Cres East BN3 43 D4
Ingram Cres West BN3 43 D4
Ingram Ct BN3 30 A4
Ingrams Av TN39 14 D1
Ingrams Way BN27 25 C8
Inhams Wood TN6 18 B2
Inkpen La RH18 22 C4
Innings Dr BN24 40 D5
Iona CI BN27 24 C3
Irelands La BN7 33 E4
Ironlatch Av TN38 50 A1
Ironstone Way TN22 53 E5
Isabel CI BN25 48 D2
Isabel Cres BN3 43 D3
Isherwood TN33 13 B2
Islingword St BN2 17 H2
Iveagh Cres BN9 36 D3
Ivory PI BN2 17 G3
Ivy La BN21 21 E1
Ivy Mews BN3 16 A3
Ivy PI BN3 16 A3
Ivy Ter BN21 21 E3

Jackies La BN8 38 A1
Jackson Mews BN9 37 C5
Jackson St BN2 17 H1
Jacobs Acre TN40 14 D5
James Av BN27 29 A1
Jameson Rd TN40 14 D5
Jardine Ct TN6 18 D4
Jarretts CI TN31 46 C3
Jasmine Grn BN27 24 D4
Jason CI BN10 39 B2
Jay Rd BN10 39 E3
Jeffreys Way TN22 52 D3
Jeffries Way TN6 18 D2
Jephson CI BN20 21 E5
Jersey St BN2 17 H2
Jesmond CI BN3 43 D4
Jesmond Rd BN3 43 D4
Jevington Dr BN26 48 C3
Jevington Gdns BN21 21 E4
Jevington Rd BN26 42 A6
Jew St BN1 17 E3
Joes La BN27 29 D2
John St BN2 17 G4
John's Cross Rd TN32 51 C6
Jonas La TN5 54 A3
Jonas La TN5 54 D2
Jubilee Gdns BN25 49 F2
Jubilee Homes BN9 37 B6
Jubilee Mews TN5 17 F3
Jubilee Rd, Bexhill TN39 14 A1
Jubilee Rd,
Brighton BN41 43 A3
Jubilee St BN1 17 F3
Juggs CI BN7 33 E5
Juggs Rd BN7 32 C6
Junction Rd,
Brighton BN1 17 E1
Junction Rd,
Eastbourne BN21 21 F2
Junction St BN26 42 D3
Juniper CI BN25 49 H4

Kammond Av BN25 49 G2
Kate Ct TN38 50 B3
Katherine Way BN25 48 D2
Keats Walk BN23 40 A6
Kedale Rd BN25 48 D3
Keere St BN7 32 A2
Keld Av TN22 53 D6
Keld CI TN22 53 D6
Keld Dr TN22 53 D6
Kemp St BN1 17 E2
Kemps Farm Rd TN6 19 F5
Kemps Way TN32 51 D4
Kendal Rd BN3 30 A4
Kenilworth Rd TN38 50 A4
Kennard Ct RH18 22 B2
Kennedy CI TN21 28 D3
Kennedy Rd TN40 15 F4
Kennedy Way BN9 37 B5
Kensington Gdns BN1 17 F3
Kensington PI BN1 17 E2
Kensington St BN1 17 F3

62

BN24 40 D2
BN9 37 C5
ay BN3 30 A2
La BN21 25 E6
La TN21 28 C2
ews BN25 49 E6
BN25 49 E6
N3 43 C2
N40 15 F4
BN2 44 A1
ay TN40 15 G3
Rye TN31 46 B3

BN25 49 E3
BN20 20 D5
TN30 50 C3
d BN25 49 F6
N25 49 H4
N25 49 G3
BN26 42 B4
ews,
N40 14 D3
ews,
ards TN38 50 A1
Av BN10 39 C3
Cl TN20 23 A2
La TN5 54 A4
Pk TN5 54 C3
Pl TN22 21 F1
Way TN40 15 E3
Way BN7 33 F2
s Mead TN6 19 H6
TN39 14 B1
Gdns TN40 15 F3
Walk BN3 43 D2
TN38 50 B4
Ter TN38 50 B4
Bank TN33 13 E3
Cl,
n BN2 44 A2
Cl,
am BN27 25 D5
Cl, Portslade-by-Sea
43 B1
Cres TN39 14 D1
Pl TN22 53 D6
Rd BN7 25 C7
Rise TN21 29 B5
Vw TN35 56 C2
Way,
s TN35 23 D3
Way,
eld TN21 28 C3
Way,
d BN25 49 G4
side Cotts TN5 51 D2
row BN20 20 C6
d,
urne BN20 20 C6
d,
BN25 49 F4
t BN20 20 D5
y Cres BN3 30 A2
Cl BN7 33 F2
Pl BN3 30 C6
Ter, Hove BN3 30 C6
Ter,
nards TN38 50 A5
Villas BN3 30 C6
y,
orough TN6 19 F4
y,
ham BN27 24 C4
ay Dr RH18 22 D2
ing Pl BN9 37 C6
ng Rd BN9 37 C6
ing Rise BN9 37 C6
g House La BN1 17 E5
urne Rd BN22 21 G2
t Rd TN6 18 B5
se Cl BN27 25 C5
p Gdns TN34 26 D1
es Rd TN38 50 A1
toria TN38 50 C5
ead Rd BN25 49 E5
an Rd BN7 33 E3
an Way BN10 39 B2
Ct BN27 25 F7
aid Pass TN31 46 C3
aid St TN31 46 C3
nede Cl TN38 50 A4
on Ct TN31 46 A3
lfe Av BN9 37 B5
s Rd TN38 50 C5
el Flds RH18 22 B3
Gro BN21 20 D2
le Cl TN38 50 B2
ham Rd TN22 52 F3
e Dr TN22 34 A2
e Furlong BN25 49 E4
e Rd TN35 27 F1
e St, Brighton BN1 16 D5

Middle St,
Hastings TN34 26 B5
Middle St, Portslade-by-sea
BN41 43 B5
Middle Way,
Hailsham BN27 29 D2
Middle Way, Lewes BN7 32 C4
Middleham Cl BN8 47 A5
Middlesex Rd TN40 15 E5
Middleton Av BN3 43 C5
Mighell St BN2 17 G4
Milcote Av BN3 30 A3
Mildmay Cl BN8 47 A2
Mildmay Rd BN7 32 D4
Milestones TN21 28 C1
Military Rd TN31 46 C2
Mill Cl, Brighton BN41 43 B1
Mill Cl, Hastings TN35 27 G1
Mill Cl, Heathfield TN21 28 B2
Mill Cl, Polegate BN26 42 B5
Mill Cl, Westfield TN35 56 C1
Mill Cres TN6 18 D3
Mill Dr,
Crowborough TN6 18 D3
Mill Dr, Hove BN3 30 B1
Mill Dr, Seaford BN25 49 F4
Mill Dro, Seaford BN25 49 F4
Mill Dro, Uckfield TN22 53 D6
Mill Gap Rd BN21 21 E1
Mill Gdns,
Heathfield TN21 28 C4
Mill Gdns, Lewes BN8 47 B4
Mill La,
Crowborough TN6 18 D3
Mill La, Hailsham BN27 24 C1
Mill La, Hastings TN35 27 G1
Mill La, Uckfield TN22 53 D6
Mill La, Westfield TN35 56 C1
Mill Mead BN8 47 B3
Mill Rd, Brighton BN41 43 A4
Mill Rd,
Eastbourne BN21 20 C6
Mill Rd, Hailsham BN27 25 E6
Mill Rd, Heathfield TN21 28 B2
Mill Rd, Lewes BN7 33 G2
Mill Rd, Ringmer BN8 47 B4
Mill Rd, Rye TN31 46 B3
Mill Rd,
Winchelsea TN36 55 A2
Mill Rise,
Heathfield TN21 28 C1
Mill Rise,
Robertsbridge TN32 51 B6
Mill View Rd TN39 14 C1
Mill Vw BN8 47 A4
Mill Way BN26 42 B5
Milland Cl TN40 15 F3
Milland Mews BN27 24 D4
Milland Rd BN27 24 D4
Millberg Rd BN25 49 H3
Millbrook Cl TN21 29 B5
Millbrook Rd TN6 18 D4
Millcross Rd BN41 43 B2
Milldown Rd BN25 49 F4
Millers Rise BN27 25 C7
Millfield Cl, Lewes BN8 38 C2
Millfield Cl,
Seaford BN25 49 G3
Millfield Rise TN40 14 D4
Millfields Ct BN26 42 C2
Millham TN39 14 A3
Millstream Gdns BN26 14 A3
Millward Rd BN24 40 D5
Millwood Cl TN22 52 D1
Millwood La TN22 52 D1
Milner Flats BN2 17 G3
Milnthorpe Gdns BN20 20 D5
Milnthorpe Rd,
Eastbourne BN20 20 D5
Milnthorpe Rd,
Hove BN3 30 A4
Milton Cres BN21 20 C1
Milton Rd BN21 20 C1
Milward Cres TN34 26 B5
Milward Rd TN34 26 B5
Mimosa Cl BN26 42 C1
Minster Cl BN26 42 C1
Mistley Cl TN40 15 H2
Mitten Rd TN40 14 D4
Moat Croft Rd BN21 20 D2
Moat La TN33 56 A3
Modena Rd BN3 30 A4
Molesworth St BN3 30 B3
Mona Rd BN21 21 G1
Monarch Gdns BN26 49 G2
Monceux Rd,
Eastbourne BN21 20 B1
Monceux Rd,
Hailsham BN27 29 A1
Monks La BN7 33 F5
Monks Walk TN36 55 A3
Monks Way, Lewes BN7 33 F1
Monks Way, Rye TN31 38 B4

Monmouth St BN3 30 C5
Montacute Rd BN7 32 C6
Montacute Way TN22 52 E4
Montague Way BN24 40 B4
Montargis Way TN6 18 D5
Montford Cl BN24 40 B3
Montford Rd BN24 40 B3
Montgomery St BN3 30 B4
Montpelier Cres BN1 16 C1
Montpelier Pl BN1 16 B2
Montpelier Rd BN1 16 B4
Montpelier St BN1 16 C3
Montpelier Ter BN1 16 C3
Montpelier Villas BN1 16 B3
Montreal Rd BN2 17 H2
Moor La, Hastings TN35 56 C2
Moor La, Lewes BN8 47 D6
Moore Pk BN27 25 F6
Moray Walk BN27 24 C4
Morgan Cl TN39 14 C1
Morlais Pl TN36 55 D3
Morlais Ridge TN36 55 D4
Morley Cl BN7 33 E6
Morley St BN2 17 G3
Morningside Cl BN25 49 E3
Mornington Cres BN3 43 D4
Mornington Mansions
BN3 43 D4
Morris Rd BN7 32 C1
Mortain Pk BN27 25 F7
Mortain Rd BN24 40 B3
Mortimer Gdns BN26 42 B5
Mortimer Rd BN3 30 B3
Moscow Rd TN35 27 E2
Motcombe La BN21 20 C1
Motcombe Rd BN21 20 C1
Mottins Hill TN6 19 H6
Mount Cl BN9 36 F4
Mount Dr BN2 45 E3
Mount Harry Rd BN7 32 C3
Mount Idol Vw TN39 14 A1
Mount Joy TN33 13 C2
Mount Pl BN7 32 A1
Mount Pleasant,
Brighton BN2 17 H4
Mount Pleasant,
Crowborough TN6 19 F6
Mount Pleasant,
Lewes BN7 32 A1
Mount Pleasant,
Wadhurst TN5 54 D2
Mount Pleasant Cres
TN34 26 B3
Mount Pleasant Ct TN34 26 C3
Mount Pleasant Rd,
Hastings TN34 26 B3
Mount Pleasant Rd,
Newhaven BN9 36 F2
Mount Rd,
Eastbourne BN20 21 E5
Mount Rd,
Hastings TN35 27 E2
Mount Rd,
Newhaven BN9 36 F4
Mount St, Battle TN33 13 C3
Mount St, Lewes BN7 33 F5
Mount View Ter BN7 25 E7
Mount Zion Pl BN1 16 D3
Mountain Ash Cl BN27 25 B3
Mountfield Rd BN7 33 F5
Mountney Dr BN24 41 G2
Mountney Rd BN21 21 F1
Moy Av BN22 20 C1
Moyne Cl BN3 43 D2
Mount Pleasant TN22 53 D6
Mulberry La BN6 35 B5
Mulberry Pk TN22 34 B2
Mulberry Way TN21 28 D4
Murray Av BN9 37 B5
Mutton Hall Hill TN21 28 C1
Mutton Hall La TN21 28 C1
Myrtle Rd TN6 18 D5

Namrik Mews BN3 30 B6
Nan Tucks La TN22 31 C6
Naomi Cl BN20 20 D4
Neaves La BN8 47 D4
Neills Cl BN9 37 C6
Nelson Pl BN2 17 G3
Nelson Rd TN34 26 B4
Nelson Row BN2 17 G3
Netherfield Rd TN33 13 B1
Nettlesworth La,
Old Heathfield TN21 28 F4
Nettlesworth La,
Vines Cross TN21 29 D4
Nevill Av, Hove BN3 30 A2
Nevill Av, Portslade-by-Sea
BN3 43 D1
Nevill Cl,
Crowborough TN6 18 A6
Nevill Cl, Hove BN3 30 B1
Nevill Cres BN3 32 D3
Nevill Ct TN6 18 A6

Nevill Gdns BN3 30 B1
Nevill Grn TN22 52 D3
Nevill Pl BN3 30 B1
Nevill Rd, Brighton BN2 44 B4
Nevill Rd,
Crowborough TN6 18 D3
Nevill Rd, Hove BN3 30 B1
Nevill Rd, Lewes BN7 32 D2
Nevill Rd, Uckfield TN22 52 D3
Nevill Way BN3 30 B1
Neville Cotts BN6 35 B6
Neville Rd,
Eastbourne BN22 21 G1
Neville Rd,
Peacehaven BN10 39 C3
New Barn Cl,
Brighton BN41 43 B1
New Barn Cl,
Hailsham BN27 25 E7
New Barn La TN22 53 D7
New Barn Rd BN2 44 A1
New Church Rd BN3 43 C4
New Cut TN35 56 C2
New Dorset St BN1 16 D3
New England La TN31 46 C1
New England St BN1 17 F1
New Lydd Rd TN31 34 A5
New Moorsite TN35 56 D3
New Par TN21 28 C1
New Park Vw TN40 14 D4
New Pl,
Eastbourne BN21 20 C2
New Pl, Uckfield TN22 53 D7
New Pond Hill TN21 28 A2
New Rd, Brighton BN1 17 E4
New Rd,
Crowborough TN6 18 D3
New Rd,
Eastbourne BN22 21 G1
New Rd, Fairlight TN35 23 B3
New Rd,
Hailsham BN27 24 D1
New Rd, Hassocks BN6 35 A6
New Rd, Hastings TN35 27 F2
New Rd,
Heathfield TN21 28 C3
New Rd, Lewes BN7 32 A2
New Rd,
Newhaven BN9 36 C2
New Rd, Polegate BN26 42 D2
New Rd, Ringmer BN8 47 A5
New Rd, Rye TN31 46 D3
New Rd, Uckfield TN22 53 D8
New Steine BN2 17 G5
New Steine Mews BN2 17 H5
New Upperton Rd BN21 20 D1
New Winchelsea Rd
TN31 46 C4
Newark Pl BN2 17 G2
Newfield La BN9 37 C6
Newfield Rd BN9 37 B5
Newgate Rd TN37 50 C2
Newhaven Heights BN9 37 C8
Newhaven Rd BN25 48 A2
Newhaven Sq*,
South Way BN9 37 C5
Newhaven St BN2 17 G1
Newick Cl BN25 49 H5
Newick Dr BN8 38 B1
Newick Hill BN8 38 C1
Newick La,
Heathfield TN21 28 E1
Newick La,
Mayfield TN20 23 B3
Newington Ct TN5 51 C2
Newlands Av TN39 14 B3
Newlands Park Way
BN8 38 C1
Newlands Pl RH18 22 C2
Newlands Rd BN2 44 C4
Newmans Way TN35 27 F1
Newnham Way TN22 28 C2
Newton Pk BN27 25 F6
Newton Rd, Lewes BN7 33 E3
Newton Rd,
Peacehaven BN10 39 C2
Newtown Rd BN3 30 C3
Nightingale Rise TN22 53 E7
Nile St BN1 17 E5
Ninfield Rd TN39 14 B1
Nizells Av BN3 16 A1
Nook Cl TN35 27 F1
Norbury Cl TN6 18 C2
Nore Rd BN9 37 A6
Norfolk Bldgs BN1 16 A4
Norfolk Cl TN39 14 C1
Norfolk Mews BN1 16 A4
Norfolk Rd BN1 16 A3
Norfolk Sq BN1 16 A4
Norfolk St BN1 16 A4
Norfolk Ter BN1 16 B2
Norfolk Way TN22 52 D4
Norlington Ct BN8 47 A2
Norlington Flds BN8 47 A2

Norlington La BN8 47 A2
Norman Cl, Battle TN33 13 E3
Norman Cl,
Seaford BN25 48 A2
Norman Rd, Hove BN3 43 D5
Norman Rd,
Newhaven BN9 37 C6
Norman Rd,
Pevensey BN24 41 E5
Norman Rd,
St Leonards TN37 50 C5
Normandale TN39 14 A5
Normansal Cl BN25 49 F2
Normansal Park Av
BN25 49 F2
North Beeches Rd TN6 19 E5
North Camp La BN25 49 E3
North Cl, Brighton BN41 43 A2
North Cl, Polegate BN26 42 D2
North Cres BN27 25 C6
North Ct BN7 32 C1
North End BN6 35 B5
North Farm Cotts BN41 43 A1
North Gdns BN1 16 D2
North Heath Cl BN27 24 E4
North La, Brighton BN41 43 A1
North La,
Newhaven BN9 37 C5
North Pl BN1 17 F3
North Quay Rd BN9 36 C4
North Rd, Bexhill TN39 14 C1
North Rd, Hastings TN35 16 D3
North Rd, Lewes BN8 47 B3
North Rd,
Pevensey BN24 41 E4
North Rd,
Polegate BN26 12 B2
North Rd, Portslade-by-Sea
BN41 43 A1
North Rd,
St Leonards TN37 50 C2
North Row TN22 52 D4
North Salts TN31 46 D2
North St, Brighton BN1 16 D4
North St,
Eastbourne BN21 21 F3
North St,
Hailsham BN27 25 D6
North St, Lewes BN7 32 B1
North St, Lower Horsebridge
BN27 24 B1
North St, Mayfield TN20 23 B1
North St, Polegate BN26 12 C2
North St, Portslade-by-Sea
BN41 43 B5
North St,
St Leonards TN38 50 C5
North St,
Windhelsea TN36 55 A2
North Street Quad BN1 16 D4
North Ter TN34 26 D3
North Trade Rd TN33 13 A3
North Way, Lewes BN7 32 C4
North Way,
Newhaven BN9 37 C5
North Way,
Seaford BN25 49 E2
Northbridge St TN32 51 C4
Northcliffe Cl BN25 49 F3
Northdown Cl BN9 37 B6
Northdown Rd BN9 37 B6
Northease Cl BN3 43 C1
Northease Dr BN3 43 C1
Northern Av BN26 42 D2
Northfield BN26 42 D4
Northfield Cl BN25 49 E2
Northfield Rise BN2 44 D3
Northgate Cl BN2 44 B3
Northiam Rd BN20,21 20 B1
Northridge TN31 38 B5
Northwood Av BN2 45 G4
Norton Cl BN3 30 C5
Norton Rd, Hove BN3 30 C5
Norton Rd,
Newhaven BN9 37 D6
Norton Ter BN9 37 D6
Norway St BN41 43 B4
Nursery Cl,
Hailsham BN27 25 E6
Nursery Cl,
Polegate BN26 42 D2
Nursery Fld TN22 31 B5
Nursery La,
Hailsham BN27 29 D2
Nursery La,
Maresfield TN22 34 B1
Nursery La,
Uckfield TN22 53 D8
Nursery Path BN27 25 D7
Nursery Way TN21 28 A2
Nutley Av BN25 45 E4
Nutley Cl TN31 46 B3
Nye Cl TN6 18 D5

Oak Rd TN40 14 C4
Oak Tree Ct TN22 52 E4
Oakfield Rd TN35 26 D2
Oakhurst Dr TN6 19 E3
Oakhurst Rd TN33 13 D1
Oaklands TN6 19 E5
Oaklands Av BN2 45 E3
Oaklands Cl BN26 42 D3
Oaklands Way BN27 25 C8
Oaklea Way TN22 53 C5
Oakleaf Dr BN26 42 C1
Oakleigh Dr TN21 28 D3
Oakmede Way BN8 47 A4
Oaktree Way BN27 24 E4
Oakwood Av TN39 14 C2
Oakwood Cl BN26 26 B1
Oakwood Dr TN22 52 F4
Oakwood Pk RH18 22 C3
Oast House Dr TN31 46 A4
Oast House Fld TN36 31 C2
Oast House Rd TN36 31 C2
Observatory Vw BN27 25 F6
Ocklye Rd TN6 18 A4
Ocklynge Av BN21 20 D1
Ocklynge Rd BN21 20 D2
Ockman La TN31 46 C3
Offa Rd TN35 27 E1
Offam Cl BN25 49 F2
Offham Rd BN7 33 E3
Offham Road BN7 32 C1
Okehurst Rd BN21 20 C2
Old Brickyard TN31 46 A3
Old Camp Rd BN20 20 B3
Old Dr BN26 42 C3
Old Farm Rd TN39 14 C3
Old Ghyll Rd TN21 28 C3
Old House Gdns TN34 26 B1
Old House La TN22 53 E8
Old Humphrey Av*,
   All Saints St TN34 26 D4
Old La,
   Crowborough TN6 18 B3
Old La, Mayfield TN20 23 A2
Old La, Poundfield TN6 19 F5
Old London Rd TN34 26 D4
Old Lydd Rd TN35 34 A5
Old Malling Way BN7 33 F2
Old Manor Cl TN40 15 E4
Old Mill Cl,
   Brighton BN41 43 A4
Old Mill Cl,
   Hailsham BN27 24 C3
Old Mill Ct TN6 18 C4
Old Mill La BN26 42 B6
Old Mill Pk TN39 14 B3
Old Mill Walk TN33 13 C3
Old Motcombe Mews
   BN21 20 C1
Old Orchard Pl BN27 25 D7
Old Orchard Rd BN21 21 E3
Old Place Mews BN2 44 B4
Old River Way TN36 55 D3
Old School Cl BN26 42 C2
Old Shoreham Rd,
   Brighton BN41 43 A3
Old Shoreham Rd,
   Hove BN3 30 A3
Old Station Rd TN5 54 D1
Old Steine BN1 17 F5
Old Swan La BN27 25 F8
Old Timbers La TN22 53 D6
Old Top Rd TN35 27 F1
Old Wish Rd BN21 21 E4
Oldaker Rd BN8 38 C1
Oldfield Av BN20 42 C5
Oldfield Cres BN27 24 D4
Oldfield Rd BN20 42 C5
Olive Rd BN3 43 D3
Oliver Cl,
   Crowborough TN6 19 E5
Oliver Cl, Hastings TN34 26 A5
Olivers Mews TN33 13 D4
Olives Mdw TN22 53 D5
Olives Yd TN22 53 D5
Onslow Rd BN3 30 D2
Orange Row BN1 17 E3
Orchard Av BN3 30 C2
Orchard Cl, Bexhill TN40 14 D4
Orchard Cl,
   Hastings TN34 26 B2
Orchard Gdns BN3 30 B2
Orchard La BN6 35 B4
Orchard Par BN20 42 C6
Orchard Rd,
   Bexhill TN40 14 D2
Orchard Rd, Hove BN3 30 B2
Orchard Rd, Lewes BN7 33 G3
Oriental Pl BN1 16 B4
Orion Cl BN27 25 F6
Osborne Cl TN34 26 A2
Osborne Hill TN6 19 G6
Osborne Rd,
   Crowborough TN6 19 G6

Osborne Rd,
   Eastbourne BN20 20 A2
Osborne Villas BN3 30 C6
Osmers Hill TN5 54 E1
Osmond Gdns BN3 16 B1
Osmond Rd BN3 16 B1
Osprey Cl BN27 25 F6
Osprey Dr I N22 53 E7
Otham Court La BN26 42 C1
Otham Pk BN27 25 F7
Otteham Cl BN26 42 D3
Ousedale Cl BN7 33 E4
Outlook Av BN10 39 F3
Over St BN1 17 E2
Oxbottom Cl BN8 38 B2
Oxendean Cl BN22 42 D6
Oxendean Gdns BN22 42 D5
Oxford Mews BN3 30 D4
Oxford Pl BN1 17 F1
Oxford Rd BN22 21 G1
Oxford Ter*,
   Tackleway TN34 26 D5

Paddock Cl TN40 14 D3
Paddock Gdns BN26 42 B5
Paddock La BN7 33 E4
Paddock Rd BN7 32 A2
Pages Av TN39 14 A6
Pages Cl TN21 28 A2
Pages Cotts TN21 28 C1
Pages Hill TN21 28 A2
Paines Twitten BN7 32 A2
Palace Pl BN1 17 F5
Palesgate La TN6 19 F2
Palma Cl BN26 42 C1
Palmeira Av BN3 30 D5
Palmeira Sq BN3 30 D5
Palmerston Rd BN9 36 F4
Pankhurst Cl TN39 14 B1
Pankhurst Rise TN39 14 B1
Paradise Cl BN20 20 C4
Paradise Dr BN20 20 C4
Park Av, Bexhill TN39 14 C6
Park Av, Hastings TN34 26 A1
Park Av, Hove BN3 30 A1
Park Av,
   Peacehaven BN10 39 A1
Park Cfr BN26 42 C5
Park Cl, Brighton BN41 43 B2
Park Cl,
   Eastbourne BN20 20 D2
Park Cl, Hailsham BN27 25 D7
Park Cres,
   Crowborough TN6 18 D3
Park Cres,
   Forest Row RH18 22 D3
Park Cres,
   Hastings TN34 50 D1
Park Cres, Portslade-by-Sea
   BN41 43 A3
Park Cres,
   Rottingdean BN2 44 B4
Park Dr, Hastings TN34 50 D1
Park Dr, Newhaven BN9 36 F3
Park Dr Cl BN9 36 F3
Park Gate,
   Hailsham BN27 24 E3
Park Gate, Hove BN3 16 A1
Park Hill BN2 17 H4
Park La, Battle TN33 13 C3
Park La, Bexhill TN39 14 B3
Park La,
   Crowborough TN6 18 D3
Park Rd, Bexhill TN39 14 C5
Park Rd, Brighton BN2 44 B4
Park Rd,
   Crowborough TN6 18 D3
Park Rd,
   Forest Row RH18 22 D3
Park Rd, Hailsham BN27 24 D1
Park Rd,
   Heathfield TN21 28 D2,3
Park Rd, Lewes BN7 33 E4
Park Rd,
   Peacehaven BN10 39 E3
Park Rd, Seaford BN25 48 C4
Park Road Ter BN2 17 H4
Park St BN2 17 H4
Park Ter BN2 44 B4
Park View Cl BN10 39 A1
Park View Rd,
   Hastings TN35 56 C1
Park View Rd,
   Hove BN3 30 C3
Park View Rd,
   Uckfield TN22 52 D3
Park View Rise BN10 39 A1
Park View Ter*,
   Cottage La TN35 56 C1
Park Vw,
   Hailsham BN27 29 A1
Park Vw, Hastings TN34 50 A1
Park Vw, Rye TN31 38 B6
Park Vw, Uckfield TN22 31 B5

Parker Ct BN41 43 B1
Parker Rd TN34 26 C2
Parkhurst Rd TN40 14 C5
Parklands TN22 34 A3
Parks Yd TN33 13 C3
Parkside TN21 28 D3
Parkside Rd BN25 49 F4
Parsonage La,
   Hastings TN35 56 A2
Parsonage La,
   Winchelsea TN36 31 C2
Parsonage Rd BN21 20 C1
Pashley Rd BN20 20 B3
Paton Rd TN39 14 A1
Paul Cl BN27 24 C3
Pavilion Bldgs BN1 17 F4
Pavilion Par BN2 17 F4
Pavilion St BN2 17 F4
Payne Av BN3 30 A3
Paynsbridge Way TN21 29 B5
Paynters Way BN8 38 C2
Peartree Fld TN36 31 C2
Pebble Rd BN24 41 F3
Pebsham Dr TN40 15 G2
Pebsham La TN40 15 F3
Peckham Cl BN7 33 F2
Peelings La BN24 40 A3
Pegler Av BN9 37 B7
Pegwell Cl TN34 26 A3
Pelham Cl BN24 40 A4
Pelham Cres,
   Hailsham BN27 25 E7
Pelham Cres,
   Hastings TN35 26 B5
Pelham Pl TN35 26 B5
Pelham Rd BN25 48 D5
Pelham Sq BN1 17 F2
Pelham St,
   Brighton BN1 17 F1
Pelham St,
   Hastings TN34 26 B5
Pelham Ter BN7 33 F4
Pelham Yd BN25 49 E5
Pell Cl TN5 54 F1
Pell Hill TN5 54 F2
Pellbrook Rd BN7 32 D2
Pellings Farm Cl TN6 19 F4
Pelwood Rd TN31 34 C6
Pembroke Av BN3 30 B5
Pembroke Cl BN27 24 E3
Pembroke Cres BN3 30 B4
Pembroke Gdns BN3 30 B5
Pembury Gro TN39 14 B2
Pendragon Ct BN3 30 B3
Pendrill Pl TN5 54 E2
Penhurst Dr TN40 15 G2
Penland Rd TN40 15 F3
Penn Rise BN8 47 B4
Pennine Rise TN34 26 D1
Penny La TN40 15 G3
Peppercombe Rd BN20 20 A2
Percy Rd TN35 27 E1
Perry Hill BN2 45 E2
Perth Cl BN25 49 H4
Peter James Cl TN31 34 B5
Peter James La TN35 23 B1
Pett Level Rd,
   Hastings TN35 23 D2
Pett Level Rd,
   Winchelsea TN36 55 C6
Pevensey Cl BN25 49 G3
Pevensey Park Rd BN24 40 A3
Pevensey Rd,
   Eastbourne BN21,22 21 G2
Pevensey Rd,
   Newhaven BN9 37 A7
Pevensey Rd,
   Polegate BN26 42 D3
Pevensey Rd,
   St Leonards TN38 50 B4
Philip Cole Cl TN34 26 C5
Phoenix Causeway TN22 32 B1
Phoenix Cl TN27 25 F6
Phoenix Pl,
   Brighton BN2 17 G1
Phoenix Pl, Lewes BN7 32 B1
Phoenix Rise BN2 17 G1
Phyllis Av BN10 39 A2
Picardy Cl TN33 13 D3
Piccadilly La TN20 23 D3
Pickforde La TN5 51 B2
Piddinghoe Av BN10 39 C3
Piddinghoe Cl BN10 39 D2
Piddinghoe Mead BN9 36 A4
Pilmer Rd TN6 18 D3
Pilot Rd TN34 26 C1
Piltdown Cl,
   Bexhill TN39 14 C4
Piltdown Cl,
   Hastings TN34 26 A4
Piltdown Rise TN22 52 E4
Pinders Rd TN35 27 E3
Pinders Walk TN35 27 F2

Pine Av TN34 26 D1
Pine Gro TN6 18 C4
Pine Tree Cl BN9 37 C6
Pine Tree Rd TN21 28 C3
Pine Walk TN22 52 E4
Pine Way BN27 25 C6
Pinewood Chase TN6 18 B3
Pinewood Cl BN25 49 F3
Pinwell Rd BN7 32 B2
Pipe Pass BN7 32 A2
Pipers Cl, Bexhill TN40 14 D4
Pipers Cl, Wadhurst TN5 54 F3
Pipers Fld TN22 53 D8
Pipers Gate TN22 53 D8
Pipit Mdw TN22 53 D7
Pippin Cl BN27 29 C2
Pitreavie Dr BN27 25 C5
Pitt Dr BN25 49 F2
Place La BN25 49 E5
Pleasant View Rd TN6 18 C2
Plemont Gdns TN39 14 B3
Plovers Barrows TN22 31 C4
Plumpton Cl TN40 14 D2
Plynlimmon Rd TN34 26 C4
Point Hill TN31 46 D2
Polegate By-Pass BN26 42 B3
Polegate Rd BN27 25 C8
Pollington Pl TN6 18 D4
Ponswood Rd TN38 50 B1
Pook Reed Cl TN21 28 B3
Pook Reed La TN21 28 A3
Pool Pas BN1 17 F5
Pool Valley BN1 17 F5
Poplar Av BN3 43 D1
Port St TN34 26 B5
Port Vw BN9 36 D3
Porters Way BN26 42 D3
Portfield Cl TN40 15 E3
Portland Av BN3 43 D4
Portland Cl BN27 24 C4
Portland Pl TN34 26 B5
Portland Rd, Hove BN3 30 A4
Portland Rd,
   Portslade-by-Sea BN43 43 C4
Portland Sq TN21 28 F2
Portland St BN1 17 E4
Portland Ter BN9 36 D3
Portland Villas BN3 43 C4
Post Horn Cl RH18 22 E4
Post Horn La RH18 22 E3
Post Office Pass*,
   High St TN34 26 C5
Potato La BN8 47 B2
Potters Fld BN8 47 B2
Potters La BN7 33 E5
Pottingfield Rd TN31 46 A3
Poundfield Farm TN6 19 F4
Poundfield Rd TN6 19 E4
Powdermill La TN33 13 D4
Powell Cl BN9 36 D4
Powell Gdns BN9 36 D3
Powell Rd BN8 38 C2
Powis Gro BN1 16 C2
Powis Rd BN1 16 C2
Powis Sq BN1 16 C2
Powis Villas BN1 16 C2
Poynings Cl BN25 49 H5
Poynter Rd BN3 30 B3
Pratts Folly La TN6 18 C5
Preston Rd TN39 14 C1
Preston St BN1 16 B4
Primmers Green Rd
   TN5 54 E2
Primrose Hill,
   Bexhill TN39 14 A3
Primrose Hill,
   Hastings TN35 23 E2
Primrose La RH18 22 D3
Prince Albert St BN1 17 E4
Prince Charles Rd BN7 33 G2
Prince Edwards Rd BN7 32 D4
Princes Av BN3 30 B5
Princes Cl BN25 48 D3
Princes Cres BN3 30 B6
Princes Pl BN1 17 E4
Princes Rd TN37 50 D4
Princes Sq BN3 30 B5
Princes St BN2 17 G1
Princess Dr BN25 48 C3
Prinsep Rd BN3 30 B3
Priory Av TN34 26 A4
Priory Cl, Hastings TN34 26 A4
Priory Cl,
   Pevensey BN24 41 E4
Priory Cres BN7 33 F5
Priory Ct BN7 33 G5
Priory La BN23 40 A6
Priory Place Flats BN7 33 F5
Priory Rd,
   Eastbourne BN23 40 A6
Priory Rd,
   Forest Row RH18 22 A4
Priory Rd,
   Hastings TN34 26 C5

Priory St, Hastings
Priory St, Lewes BN
Priory Ter TN34
Prospect Gdns BN2
Prospect Pl TN34
Prospect Rd TN21
Providence Pl BN1
Providence Way TN3
Pudding Cake La TN
Putlands Cres TN39

Quantock Gdns TN3
Quarry Cotts TN5
Quarry Cres TN34
Quarry Hill TN38
Quarry Ho TN38
Quarry La BN25
Quarry Rd,
   Hastings TN34
Quarry Rd,
   Newhaven BN9
Quarry Ter TN34
Quebec Cl TN39
Quebec St BN2
Queen Annes Cl BN7
Queen Sq BN1
Queens App TN22
Queens Cotts TN5
Queens Dr TN22
Queens Gdns,
   Brighton BN1
Queens Gdns,
   Eastbourne BN21
Queens Gdns,
   Hove BN3
Queens Par BN3
Queens Par*,
   York Gardens TN34
Queens Park Gdns
   BN25
Queens Park Rd BN2
Queens Pl, Brighton B
Queens Pl, Hove BN3
Queens Rd,
   Brighton BN1
Queens Rd,
   Crowborough TN6
Queens Rd,
   Hailsham BN27
Queens Rd,
   Hastings TN34
Queens Rd, Lewes BN
Queens Road Quad BN
Queens Sq TN34
Queensbury Mews BN
Queensway BN25
Quickbourne La TN31
Quinnell Dr BN27
Quinton Cl BN27

Railway App BN9
Railway La BN7
Railway Rd BN9
Railway St BN1
Ranalah Est BN9
Ranelagh Villas BN3
Rannoch Rd TN6
Rannoch Rd West TN6
Ranscombe Hill BN8
Raphael Rd BN3
Rapsons Rd BN20
Rattle Rd BN24
Ratton Rd BN21
Raven Ct TN33
Ravenscroft BN20
Ravine Cl TN34
Rayford Cl BN10
Rayford Ct TN40
Raymond Cl BN25
Rectory Cl,
   Eastbourne BN20
Rectory Cl, Hove BN3
Rectory Cl,
   Newhaven BN9
Rectory Cl,
   St Leonards TN38
Rectory La, Rye TN31
Rectory La,
   Winchelsea TN36
Rectory Rd BN9
Rectory Way TN40
Red Barn Mews TN3
Red Lake Ter TN35
Redbrook La TN22
Redmayne Dr TN22
Redoubt Rd BN22
Redshank Ct BN27
Regency Cl TN22
Regency Gdns BN
Regency Mews,
   Brighton BN1
Regency Mews,
   Eastbourne BN20
Regency Rd East BN1

West BN1 16 C4
BN1 16 B4
BN1 17 E5
BN1 16 C3
21 28 C1
v BN1 16 D3
TN31 46 C3
BN1 17 E3
BN25 48 D3
d TN39 14 C5
r TN40 15 E3
d BN3 30 A4
own La BN26 42 B3
Rd BN3 30 A5
Way BN25 49 G3
TN35 27 F1
Gdns TN20 23 B1
Av TN39 14 A6
CITN39 14 A6
Gdns BN2 17 G1
GroTN39 14 A6
Par BN2 17 G2
Pl,
BN2 17 G2
Pl,
rne BN21 21 E2
Rd,
TN39 14 B6
Rd,
ey BN24 41 E4
Rd,
BN25 48 D5
St,
n BN2 17 G2
St,
sTN34 26 D3
Ter,
n BN2 17 G1
Ter,
BN25 48 D4
ltTN39 14 A4
ds Cl BN20 20 B2
CITN21 28 C1
od Av BN24 45 E6
od CITN22 53 E8
od Gdns TN40 15 F4
d BN3 30 D3
Rd,
BN8 33 H2
Rd,
ven BN9 37 A7
Rd,
BN25 49 E6
d Rd TN39 14 D2
hase BN21 20 D2
BN26 12 C2
y TN22 53 D6
e BN7 17 F3
e,
Row RH18 22 B2
e,
aven BN9 37 D5
e Gdns TN6 19 G6
StBN1 17 F3
ressell CITN34 26 A3
ill TN36 55 A2
on Pass*,
tson StTN34 26 A5
on StTN34 26 A6
on Ter TN34 26 A6
ons Hill TN34 26 D3
CITN22 34 B3
Post La BN27 25 B8
Row BN41 43 A4
on Rd BN9 37 C5
ough Cl BN21 21 F1
ster Cl BN20 20 B5
ster Ho TN6 19 F5
d RdTN37 50 C1
ster Way TN6 19 F5
rd Way BN25 48 A2
ans Way TN6 19 E6
hannel EastTN31 46 D3
hannel Quay
46 C4
m Cotts BN27 29 D2
BN2 17 H5
r BN27 24 B3
ore RdTN34 26 C5
ton Way TN6 19 F5
ds La TN35 27 E4
ead RdTN35 23 E3
Park RdTN22 53 B5
dTN22 53 A5
ck Av BN10 39 B1,3
ll Av BN25 49 H5
ll Rd BN25 49 H5
ll TN6 19 G5
ck StTN34 26 C5
an Cl,
hill TN39 14 B3
an Cl,
ford BN25 49 G3
an Cft BN21 20 D1

Roman Cl BN25 48 A1
Roman Rd BN3 43 D5
Roman Way TN22 53 E5
Romans Way BN24 40 A3
Romany Cl BN41 43 B3
Romany Cl BN25 49 H4
Romney Av BN2 44 C4
Romney Rd BN2 44 C4
Rookery Cl BN9 36 E3
Rookery La TN36 55 B2
Rookery Way,
Newhaven BN9 36 E3
Rookery Way,
Seaford BN25 48 A2
Rookhurst RdTN40 15 G4
Rope Walk,
Hailsham BN27 25 D5
Rope Walk, Rye TN31 46 C3
Rope Walk ArcTN40 46 C3
Rose Walk BN25 49 E3
Rose Walk Cl BN9 37 B6
Rosehill Gdns TN6 19 G5
Roselands TN39 14 A3
Roselands Av TN20 23 A3
Rosemary Cl BN10 39 C1
Rosemary La TN35 23 B1
Rosemount Cl BN25 48 A1
Rosetti Rd BN24 41 E5
Rothbury Rd BN3 43 D4
Rother CtTN39 14 C3
Rother Rd BN25 49 F5
Rotherfield Av,
Bexhill TN40 15 E4
Rotherfield Av,
Hastings TN34 26 D3
Rotherfield La TN31 23 A1
Rotherfield RdTN6 19 H6
Rothermead TN20 23 A3
RotherviewTN32 51 D4
Rothsay RdTN38 50 C4
Rothwell Ct BN9 37 A6
Rotten Row BN7 33 E5
Rough Brow BN25 49 F3
Roundacres Way TN40 15 F3
Roundhay Av BN10 39 E3
Rowan Av BN3 43 D2
Rowan Cl,
Heathfield TN21 28 C4
Rowan Cl,
Seaford BN25 49 H4
Rowan Gdns TN40 15 F3
Rowan Way BN2 44 A1
Rowans Ct BN7 33 E4
Rowbarns TN33 13 C1
Rowe Av BN10 39 A2
Rowe Av North BN10 39 B1
Rowsley Rd BN20 20 C6
Royal Dr BN25 49 E1
Royal Military Rd TN36 55 B2
Royal Oak Mews TN20 23 R1
Royal Par BN2 21 G2
Royles Cl BN2 44 C3
Royston Gdns TN40 15 F3
Rue De Bayeux TN33 13 C3
Rufus Cl BN7 33 E4
Rugby Cl BN25 49 G3
Rusbridge La BN7 32 C1
Rushey Cl BN8 47 B3
Ruskin Rd BN3 30 A4
Russell Cotts BN21 20 D1
Russell Ct*,
George StTN34 26 C5
Russell Mews BN1 16 C4
Russell Pl BN1 16 D4
Russell Rd BN1 16 C4
Russell Row BN7 33 F2
Russell Sq BN1 16 C4
Russell St TN34 26 B5
Russett Way BN27 29 C1
Rutland Gdns BN3 30 B5
Rutland Rd BN3 30 B4
Rutley Cl TN32 51 D4
Rye Cl, Brighton BN2 45 G3
Rye Cl, Seaford BN25 49 H3
Rye Hill TN31 46 C2
Rye RdTN35 27 E1
Rylstone Rd BN22 21 H1
Ryst Wood Rd RH18 22 E3

Sackville Cl BN7 33 E4
Sackville Gdns BN3 30 Ab
Sackville Rd,
Bexhill TN39 14 C5
Sackville Rd,
Hailsham BN27 25 E7
Sackville Rd, Hove BN3 30 B3
Sadlers Way BN8 47 A4
Saffron Gdns BN26 12 B2
Saffrons Ct BN20 20 D3
Saffrons Pk BN20 20 D4
Saffrons Rd BN21 21 E2
St Andrews Cl BN21 24 B4
St Andrews Dr BN25 48 A3
St Andrews La BN7 32 A2
St Andrews Rd TN40 14 C3

St Andrews Sq TN34 26 B5
St Annes Cl TN40 15 E3
St Annes Cres BN7 33 E5
St Annes Rd,
Eastbourne BN21 20 D1
St Annes Rd, Lower
Willingdon BN22 42 D6
St Antonys BN8 47 C3
St Aubyns BN3 30 C6
St Aubyns Cres BN41 43 A4
St Aubyns Gdns BN3 30 B6
St Aubyns Mead BN2 44 C4
St Aubyns Rd,
Eastbourne BN22 21 G2
St Aubyns Rd,
Portslade-by-Sea BN41 43 A4
St Aubyns Rd,
Portslade-by-Sea BN41 43 B4
St Aubyns South BN3 30 B6
St Augustines Cl TN39 14 A6
St Boswells Cl BN27 25 B5
St Brelades BN21 21 G3
St Catherine CITN39 50 D3
St Catherines Ter BN3 30 C6
St Crispians BN25 48 D4
St Davids Av TN40 14 D4
St Denys Vw TN6 19 E5
St Dominic CITN38 50 A4
St Elizabeths BN25 49 E3
St Francis Chase TN39 14 B3
St Georges Mews BN1 17 F2
St Georges Pl BN1 17 F2
St Georges Rd,
Bexhill TN40 14 C3
St Georges Rd,
Eastbourne BN22 21 G1
St Georges Rd,
Hastings TN34 26 C3
St Giles Cl TN36 55 A3
St Gregory Cl BN20 20 D5
St Helens Av TN34 26 A1
St Helens Cres TN34 26 A1
St Helens Ct TN34 26 A1
St Helens Downs TN34 26 B1
St Helens Park RdTN34 26 A1
St Helens RdTN34 50 D1
St Heliers Av BN3 30 A4
St James Av TN40 14 D2
St James Cl TN40 14 D2
St James Cres TN40 14 D2
St James Rd,
Bexhill TN40 14 D2
St James Rd,
Eastbourne BN22 21 G1
St James Rd,
Hastings TN34 26 B4
St James St BN7 33 F5
St James's Av BN2 17 H5
St James's Pl BN2 17 F5
St James's Street Mews
BN2 17 G5
St Johns Cl TN6 18 C3
St Johns Dr BN24 40 A3
St Johns Hill BN7 32 A1
St Johns Mount BN2 17 H4
St Johns Pl,
Brighton BN2 17 H4
St Johns Pl, Hove BN3 30 D5
St Johns Rd,
Bexhill TN40 14 D2
St Johns Rd,
Crowborough TN6 18 B2
St Johns Rd,
Eastbourne BN20 20 D6
St Johns Rd, Hove BN3 30 D6
St Johns Rd,
Polegate BN26 42 C3
St Johns Rd,
St Leonards TN37 50 C4
St Johns Rd,
Seaford BN25 48 D5
St Johns St BN7 32 A1
St Johns Ter BN7 32 A1
St Josephs Cl BN3 30 B3
St Keyna Av BN3 43 C5
St Lawrence RdTN39 14 C2
St Leonards Av BN3 43 C5
St Leonards Cl BN9 36 F3
St Leonards Cl TN38 50 A5
St Leonards Gdns BN3 43 C5
St Leonards Pl BN20 20 B2
St Leonards Rd,
Bexhill TN40 14 D5
St Leonards Rd,
Eastbourne BN21 21 E2
St Leonards Rd,
Hove BN3 43 C5
St Leonards Rd,
Newhaven BN9 36 F3
St Leonards Ter BN26 42 B2
St Margarets BN2 44 C4
St Margarets Pl BN1 16 C4
St Margarets RdTN37 50 C5

St Margarets Rise BN25 48 A1
St Margarets Ter,
RyeTN31 46 C4
St Margarets Ter,
St Leonards TN37 50 D4
St Martins Cres BN9 36 D3
St Martins La BN7 32 A2
St Mary-in-the-Fields
TN20 23 B1
St Marys Av BN27 25 E6
St Marys Cl TN5 51 B2
St Marys Garth TN22 31 B4
St Marys La,
Bexhill TN39 14 A1
St Marys La,
Wadhurst TN5 51 B2
St Marys Pl BN2 17 H5
St Marys Rd,
Eastbourne BN21 20 C1
St Marys Rd,
Hastings TN34 26 C3
St Marys Tor,
Battle TN33 13 E4
St Marys Ter,
Hastings TN34 26 C4
St Marys Villas TN33 13 E4
St Marys Walk BN27 25 D6
St Matthews DrTN38 50 C2
St Matthews Gdns TN38 50 B2
St Matthews RdTN38 50 B2
St Mellion Cl BN27 25 B5
St Michaels Cl TN6 19 F6
St Michaels Pl BN1 16 C2
St Michaels Rd BN41 43 A4
St Michaels Ter BN7 33 F3
St Nicholas Cl BN24 40 D3
St Nicholas La BN7 32 B2
St Nicholas Rd,
Brighton BN1 16 D3
St Nicholas Rd,
Portslade-by-Sea BN41 43 B4
St Pancras Gdns BN7 33 E5
St Pancras Rd BN7 33 E5
St Patricks Cres TN40 14 D3
St Patricks Rd BN3 30 B4
St Pauls Ct TN37 50 D4
St Pauls Pl TN37 50 D4
St Pauls RdTN37 50 C3
St Peters Av BN10 45 H5
St Peters Cl, Hove BN3 30 B1
St Peters Cl,
Seaford BN25 49 E3
St Peters Cres TN40 14 D3
St Peters Ct TN40 15 E4
St Peters Pl BN1 17 F1
St Peters Pl*,
High St BN7 33 E5
St Peters Rd,
St Leonards TN37 50 C2
St Peters Rd,
Seaford BN25 49 E2
St Peters St BN1 17 F1
St Philips Mews BN3 30 A5
St Raphaels TN22 31 C4
St Richards Flat BN41 43 B4
St Richards Rd BN41 43 A4
St Swithuns La BN7 32 A2
St Swithuns Ter BN7 32 A2
St Thomas of Canterbury Ct
TN20 23 B1
St Thomas St TN36 55 B2
St Thomas's RdTN34 26 C4
St Vincents Pl BN20 20 D4
St Wilfreds Pl BN25 49 G5
St Wilfrids Grn BN27 25 D5
Salehurst Rd BN21 20 C2
Salisbury Rd,
Bexhill TN40 14 C4
Salisbury Rd,
Eastbourne BN20 20 B5
Salisbury Rd, Hove BN3 30 D5
Salisbury Rd,
St Leonards TN37 50 C2
Salisbury Rd,
Seaford BN25 48 D4
Saltcote La TN31 46 C1
Saltdean Dr BN2 44 D4
Saltdean Park Rd BN2 44 D4
Saltdean Vale BN2 45 E4
Salters La TN34 26 C4
Saltwood Rd BN25 49 H3
Salvington Cres TN34 14 A4
San Jose TN35 27 E3
Sancroft Rd BN20 20 A2
Sandbanks Cl BN27 25 C8
Sandbanks Gdns BN27 25 C8
Sandbanks Gro BN27 25 D8
Sandbanks Rd BN27 25 C8
Sandbanks Way BN27 25 D7
Sandgate Cl BN25 49 H3
Sandore Cl BN25 49 G4
Sandore Rd BN25 49 G4

Sandown RdTN35 27 E2
Sandown Way TN40 15 F3
Sandridge TN6 18 C5
Sandringham Cl BN25 49 F2
Sandrock Hill TN36 55 A3
Sandwich DrTN38 50 A3
Sandy Cross Cotts TN21 28 C4
Sandy Cross La TN21 28 C4
Saunders Cl,
Hastings TN34 26 B3
Saunders Cl,
Uckfield TN22 52 B4
Saunders Way TN31 34 C6
Saxby RdTN39 14 B4
Saxon Cl BN2 45 E2
Saxon CtTN37 50 C3
Saxon Grnd BN21 20 D1
Saxon La BN25 49 E5
Saxon Rd,
Hastings TN35 27 E2
Saxon Rd, Hove BN3 43 D5
Saxon Rd,
Newhaven BN9 37 C6
Saxon Rise TN40 15 F4
Saxon StTN37 50 C5
Saxonbury CITN6 18 D4
Saxonwood RdTN33 13 C3
Sayerland Rd BN26 42 C1
Scanlan Cl BN22 42 D6
Scarletts CITN22 53 C5
School Hill,
Uckfield TN22 34 B3
School Hill,
Winchelsea TN36 55 A2
School La, Brighton BN2 45 E3
School La,
Crowborough TN6 18 D5
School La,
Forest Row RH18 22 C3
School La,
Polegate BN26 42 C2
School La, St Johns TN6 18 B2
School Pl TN40 15 G4
School Rd,
Hastings TN35 27 E2
School Rd, Hove BN3 30 A4
School Ter TN32 51 D4
Schwerte Way TN37 26 A6
Scotland St BN2 17 H2
Scott Rd BN3 30 A4
Scotts Acre TN31 34 B5
Scutes CITN34 26 B2
Sea Rd, Bexhill TN40 14 D6
Sea Rd, Hastings TN35 23 E2
Sea Rd, Pevensey BN24 41 E4
Sea Rd, Rye TN31 34 B6
Sea Rd,
St Leonards TN38 50 A5
Sea Rd,
Winchelsea TN36 55 B2
Seabourne Rd TN40 15 F2
Seacliffe BN10 45 G6
Seafield Cl BN25 49 G3
Seafield Rd BN3 30 C6
Seaford Rd, Hove BN3 43 C5
Seaford Rd,
Newhaven BN9 36 E4
Seaford Rd,
Seaford BN25 48 A1
Seagrave Cl, Lewes BN7 33 E3
Seagrave Cl,
Seaford BN25 48 A1
Seagrove Way BN25 49 F2
Searle Av BN10 39 F3
Seaside BN22 21 G2
Seaside Rd BN21 21 G3
Seaview Av BN10 39 D3
Seaview Rd,
Newhaven BN9 36 E4
Seaview Rd,
Peacehaven BN10 39 F4
Seaview Ter TN36 31 B2
Seaville Dr BN24 41 F4
Second Av, Bexhill TN40 15 G3
Second Av, Hove BN3 30 D6
Second Av,
Newhaven BN9 37 B6
Second Av, Rye TN31 34 B6
Second Rd RN10 39 A2
Sedgebrook Gdns TN34 50 D1
Sedgewick RdTN40 14 D2
Sedlescombe Gdns
TN38 50 B1
Sedlescombe Rd North
TN37 50 B1
Sedlescombe Rd South
TN38 50 B2
Sefton Chase TN6 19 E3
Sefton Way TN6 19 E3
Selborne Pl BN3 30 D4
Selborne Rd BN3 30 D5
Selby Gdns TN22 53 E7
Selby Rd TN22 53 E6
Selby Rise TN22 53 D7

Selmeston Cl TN34 50 D2
Selwyn Dr BN21 20 D1
Selwyn Rd BN21 20 D1
Senlac Ct TN33 13 C2
Senlac Gdns TN33 13 E4
Senlac Grn TN22 52 E4
Senlac Rd BN9 37 C5
Seven Sisters Rd BN22 42 D6
Sewell Av TN40 14 C3
Seymour Villas TN34 26 B2
Shakespeare St BN3 30 B3
Shalesbrook La RH18 22 D4
Sharpthorne Cres BN41 43 B2
Shawfield TN6 19 F4
Sheen Rd BN21 21 G1
Sheep Pen La BN25 49 G4
Sheep Plain TN6 18 B6
Sheep Walk BN2 44 A2
Sheepfair BN7 32 D3
Sheepsetting La TN21 28 A2
Sheiling Rd TN6 18 C3
Shelldale Av BN41 43 A4
Shelldale Cres BN41 43 A4
Shelldale Rd BN41 43 A4
Shelley Cl BN7 33 E4
Shelley Rd, Hove BN3 30 B4
Shelley Rd, Lewes BN8 47 B3
Shepham Av BN2 45 E4
Shepherd Ct*,
  Shepherd St TN38 50 C5
Shepherd St TN38 50 C5
Shepherds Cl,
  Lewes BN8 47 B3
Shepherds Cl,
  Newhaven BN9 36 A3
Shepherds Ct TN35 23 D3
Shepherds Walk TN6 19 F5
Shepherds Way,
  Hastings TN35 23 D3
Shepherds Way,
  Lewes BN8 47 B4
Shepherds Way,
  Uckfield TN22 53 D7
Sheppard Pl TN33 13 C2
Sheppey Walk BN27 24 B3
Sheraton Cl BN21 21 E3
Sheridan Ter BN3 30 B3
Sherwood Cl TN34 26 B3
Sherwood Grn BN27 25 D8
Sherwood Rd BN25 49 E3
Sherwood Rise BN25 49 E4
Ship St, Brighton BN1 17 E5
Ship St, Newhaven BN9 37 C5
Ship Street Gdns BN1 17 E5
Shipyard La TN31 46 E1
Shirlea Vw TN33 13 D3
Shirley Cl BN3 30 C1
Shirley Dr BN3 30 D3
Shirley Rd BN3 30 D3
Shirley St BN3 30 C4
Shirleys BN6 35 C6
Short Brow BN25 49 F3
Short Brow Cl BN22 42 D6
Short La BN26 12 C2
Shortdean Pl BN21 20 C1
Sidley Grn TN39 14 D2
Sidley Rd BN22 21 H1
Sidley St TN39 14 C1
Silchester Rd TN38 50 C4
Sillwood Pl BN1 16 B4
Sillwood Rd BN1 16 B4
Sillwood St BN1 16 A4
Sillwood Ter BN1 16 B3
Silva Cl TN40 15 G2
Silver La BN25 48 C1
Silverdale Ct BN27 25 D5
Silverdale Rd BN20 20 D4
Silverlands Rd TN37 50 B1
Silvester Rd TN40 14 D3
Simons Cl TN6 19 E5
Sinnock Sq*,
  High St TN34 26 C5
Slindon Av BN10 39 C3
Sloc La BN26 12 C2
Smeatons La TN36 55 D4
Smugglers Cl BN26 12 B2
Smugglers La TN6 18 B1
Smugglers Way TN35 23 D3
Snape Vw TN5 54 E4
Snatts Rd TN22 52 C4
Solway BN27 24 C3
South Cl,
  Hailsham BN27 25 D7
South Cl,
  Pevensey BN24 41 G3
South Cliff, Bexhill TN39 14 A6
South Cliff,
  Eastbourne BN20 21 E5
South Cliff Av BN20 21 E4
South Cliff Twr BN20 21 E5
South Cliffe BN7 32 C1
South Coast Rd BN2,10 48 D4
South Downs Rd BN7 33 G3
South La BN9 37 C5

South Lynn Dr BN21 21 E1
South Place Flats BN7 32 A1
South Rd,
  Hailsham BN27 25 C7
South Rd,
  Newhaven BN9 37 C6
South Rough BN8 38 C2
South St, Brighton BN1 16 D5
South St,
  Crowborough TN6 18 D5
South St,
  Eastbourne BN21 21 E3
South St,
  Hassocks BN6 35 B5
South St, Lewes BN7 32 C1
South St, Mayfield TN20 23 B1
South St, Mayfield TN20 23 C2
South St, Portslade-by-Sea
  BN41 43 A2
South St,
  St Leonards TN37 50 C4
South St, Seaford BN25 49 E5
South Ter,
  Hastings TN34 26 B4
South Ter,
  Westfield TN35 56 C2
South Undercliff TN31 46 C4
South View Rd TN5 54 E2
South Way, Lewes BN7 32 C4
South Way,
  Newhaven BN9 37 C5
South Way,
  Seaford BN25 49 A5
Southampton St BN2 17 H2
Southcourt Av TN39 14 A6
Southdown Av,
  Brighton BN41 43 B3
Southdown Av,
  Eastbourne BN20 42 C6
Southdown Av,
  Hastings TN34 26 D2
Southdown Av,
  Lewes BN7 32 D5
Southdown Av,
  Peacehaven BN10 39 D3
Southdown Cl BN9 37 A7
Southdown Ct BN27 25 E6
Southdown Pl BN7 33 G3
Southdown Rd,
  Brighton BN41 43 A1
Southdown Rd,
  Newhaven BN9 37 B6
Southdown Rd,
  Seaford BN25 49 F4
Southerden Cl BN27 25 E6
Southern Av BN26 42 D2
Southern By-Pass BN7 32 B6
Southfield BN26 42 B4
Southfields TN5 54 E1
Southfields Rd BN21 21 E2
Southlands Av TN39 14 B1
Southlands Rd TN39 14 B1
Southmead TN39 14 B1
Southover High St BN7 33 E5
Southover Pl TN7 17 G1
Southover Rd BN7 32 A2
Southover St BN2 17 G1
Southridge Rd TN6 18 C6
Southridge Rise TN6 18 C6
Southview Rd,
  Crowborough TN6 18 B6
Southview Rd,
  Peacehaven BN10 39 B1
Southwater Rd TN37 50 C3
Southway Cl TN6 18 C5
Southwood Cl TN38 50 B2
Sovereign Cl BN25 49 F2
Sovereign Mews TN38 50 A5
Sparrows Green Rd TN5 54 E3
Sparrows Grn*,
  Sparrows Green Rd
  TN5 54 E2
Spatham La BN6 35 D6
Spencer Rd BN21 21 F3
Spences Fld BN7 33 G3
Spences La BN7 33 G3
Spital Rd BN7 32 D4
Spotted Cow La TN5 31 D4
Sprays La TN33 56 A1
Spring Bank TN21 28 D1
Spring Gdns,
  Brighton BN1 17 E3
Spring Gdns, Lewes BN7 32 B1
Spring Hill TN3 38 B4
Spring Mdw RH18 22 C4
Spring St BN1 16 C3
Spring Steps TN36 55 B2
Springett Av BN8 47 B4
Springfield Av BN10 45 G5
Springfield Cl,
  Crowborough TN6 19 F4

Springfield Cl,
  Pevensey BN24 40 A3
Springfield Ct TN31 46 B1
Springfield Rd,
  Bexhill TN40 14 C3
Springfield Rd,
  Eastbourne BN22 21 G1
Springfield Rd,
  St Leonards TN38 50 B2
Springfield Valley Rd
  TN38 50 B2
Springfields TN5 51 C2
Springhead Way TN6 18 C6
Springwood Rd TN21 28 B1
Spur Rd BN26 42 D4
Spurway Pk BN26 42 D4
Stablefield TN35 56 C2
Stables La BN21 21 E3
Stafford Rd BN25 49 E4
Stainsby St TN37 50 C4
Stamford Ct TN35 27 E3
Stan La BN27 29 A1
Stanford Cl BN3 30 D2
Stanhope Pl TN38 50 C5
Stanley Rd,
  Brighton BN41 43 A3
Stanley Rd,
  Eastbourne BN22 21 G1
Stanley Rd,
  Hastings TN34 26 A4
Stanley St BN2 17 H3
Stanmer Av BN2 45 F2
Stansfield Rd BN7 33 E3
Stansted Rd BN22 21 F1
Stapley Rd BN3 43 D3
Star La, Heathfield TN21 28 F4
Star La, Mayfield TN20 23 C2
Star La, Polegate BN26 12 C2
Star Mews TN20 23 B1
Star Rd BN21 20 D2
Starfield TN6 18 C5
Starrs Green La TN33 13 F4
Starrs Grn TN33 13 E4
Starrs Mead TN33 13 F4
Station App, Battle TN33 13 E4
Station App,
  Hastings TN34 26 A5
Station App,
  Heathfield TN21 28 C2
Station App, Hove BN3 30 C4
Station App,
  Mayfield TN20 23 A2
Station App, Rye TN31 46 C3
Station App,
  St Leonards TN37 50 C4
Station App,
  Seaford BN25 48 D4
Station Rd, Bexhill TN40 14 D5
Station Rd,
  Brighton BN41 43 B6
Station Rd,
  Crowborough TN6 19 G6
Station Rd,
  Forest Row RH18 22 C2
Station Rd,
  Hailsham BN27 25 D6
Station Rd,
  Hastings TN34 26 B5
Station Rd,
  Heathfield TN21 28 C2
Station Rd,
  Hellingley BN27 24 C1
Station Rd, Lewes BN7 32 B2
Station Rd,
  Mayfield TN20 23 A2
Station Rd,
  Newhaven BN9 36 E4
Station Rd, Newick BN8 34 A2
Station Rd,
  Polegate BN26 42 C2
Station Rd,
  Robertsbridge TN32 51 C6
Station Rd, Rye TN31 38 B5
Station Rd,
  Seaford BN25 48 B3
Station Rd,
  Wadhurst TN5 54 A1
Station Rd,
  Winchelsea TN36 55 A1
Station St, Brighton BN1 17 E1
Station St,
  Eastbourne BN21 21 F3
Station St, Lewes BN7 32 A2
Staveley Rd BN20 20 D5
Steellands Rise TN5 51 C2
Steine Gdns BN21 17 F4
Steine St BN2 17 F5
Stephens Cl BN8 47 A3
Stevens Cl TN39 14 D2
Stevens St BN3 43 D4
Stevenson Cl BN23 40 A6
Stewards Inn La BN7 32 A2
Steyne Cl BN25 49 E5

Steyne Rd BN25 48 D5
Steyning Av BN10 39 B3
Steyning Cl BN25 49 H5
Steyning Rd,
  Brighton BN2 44 B4
Steyning Rd,
  Seaford BN25 49 H5
Stirling Av BN25 49 H4
Stirling Cl BN25 49 H4
Stirling Pl BN3 30 B5
Stock Dale TN35 23 D3
Stockleigh Rd TN38 50 C4
Stoke Cl BN25 49 G4
Stoke Manor Cl BN25 49 G4
Stone Cross TN20 23 A2
Stone Cross Rd TN5 54 F4
Stone St, Brighton BN1 16 B5
Stone St, Hastings TN34 26 B5
Stonebridge La TN5 54 D1
Stonecott Cl TN6 18 D6
Stonedene Cl RH18 22 E3
Stonefield Rd TN34 26 B5
Stonegate Way TN21 28 D1
Stoneham Cl BN7 33 F2
Stoneham Rd BN3 30 A4
Stonehouse Dr TN38 50 A1
Stonepark Dr RH18 22 E3
Stonestile La TN35 56 D3
Stonewood Cl BN25 49 H4
Stoney La BN27 25 E6
Storrington Cl BN3 43 D1
Straight Half Mile TN22 34 B2
Strand TN31 46 C3
Strand Hill TN36 55 B2
Stratheden Ct BN25 48 D5
Strawberry Flds TN31 38 A5
Stream La TN35 23 F2
Streamside Cl TN34 26 A2
Streatfield Gdns TN21 28 B1
Streatfield Rd,
  Heathfield TN21 28 B1
Streatfield Rd,
  Uckfield TN22 53 B5
Streele Vw TN22 52 E4
Stroma Gdns BN27 24 B3
Strome Ho TN39 14 D2
Strongs Pass*,
  All Saints St TN34 26 D5
Strood Rd TN37 50 C4
Sturdee Pl TN34 26 C5
Sturton Pl BN27 25 D6
Suffolk Rd TN39 14 C2
Suffolk St BN3 30 B4
Summer Cl BN41 43 A4
Summer Ct BN27 25 C6
Summer Hill TN38 50 A3
Summer Hill Rd BN25 14 A3
Summerdale Rd BN3 43 D1
Summerdown Cl BN20 20 C2
Summerdown Rd BN20 20 C2
Summerfields Av BN27 25 C5
Summerheath Rd BN27 25 D5
Sun St BN7 32 A1
Sunningdale Cl,
  Bexhill TN40 15 E4
Sunningdale Cl,
  Seaford BN25 49 F6
Sunningdale Ct BN27 24 C4
Sunninghill Av BN3 30 A1
Sunninghill Cl BN3 43 D1
Sunnybank Cl TN20 23 C2
Sunnybrooke Cl TN22 53 E5
Sunset Cl BN24 41 G3
Sunstar La BN26 42 A3
Sunview Av BN10 39 D3
Surrey Cl BN25 48 C3
Surrey Rd BN25 48 C3
Surrey St BN1 17 E2
Susans Rd BN21 21 F2
Sussex Av BN27 25 C6
Sussex Cl, Bexhill TN39 14 A4
Sussex Cl,
  Hailsham BN27 25 C6
Sussex Heights BN1 16 C4
Sussex Pl BN2 17 G2
Sussex Rd, Hove BN3 30 C6
Sussex Rd,
  St Leonards TN38 50 A5
Sussex St BN2 17 G3
Sussex Ter BN2 17 G3
Sussex Way BN10 45 H6
Sutherland Av TN39 14 B4
Sutherland Cl TN39 14 A4
Sutton Av,
  Peacehaven BN10 39 B2
Sutton Av,
  Seaford BN25 49 F5
Sutton Av North BN10 39 B1
Sutton Croft La BN25 49 E5
Sutton Dro BN25 49 E4
Sutton Park Rd BN25 49 E5
Sutton Pl TN40 15 F5
Sutton Rd,
  Eastbourne BN21 21 F2

Sutton Rd,
  Seaford BN25 48 C3
Swaines Pass*,
  All Saints St TN34 26 D5
Swaines Way TN21 28 D1
Swallow Ct TN22 52 E4
Swallow Dr TN33 13 E4
Swan Rd BN27 24 B3
Swan Ter TN34 26 B2
Swift Cl,
  Crowborough TN6 19 F4
Swift Cl, Uckfield TN. 53 E5
Sybron Way TN6 19 E5
Sycamore Cl,
  Heathfield TN21 28 D1
Sycamore Cl,
  St Leonards TN38 50 A5
Sycamore Cl,
  Seaford BN25 49 F6
Sycamore Ct TN22 52 E4
Sycamore Dr BN27 24 B3
Sydney Rd BN22 21 G1
Sydney St BN1 17 E2
Symbister Rd BN41 43 A2
Tackleway TN34 26 C5
Taddington Rd BN22 21 F1
Tainters Brook TN22 53 F5
Talbot Ter BN7 32 A2
Talland Par*,
  High St BN25 49 E5
Tamplin Ter BN2 17 G1
Tamworth Rd BN3 30 B3
Tandridge Rd BN3 43 D3
Tanners Brook BN7 33 G3
Tanners Way TN6 19 F5
Tanyard Cotts TN36 55 B2
Tanyard La TN36 55 B2
Tapsells La TN5 54 E3
Tarner Rd BN2 17 G2
Tarring Cl BN9 37 A7
Tas Combe Dr BN20 21 E5
Teg Cl BN41 43 A4
Telscombe Cliffs Way
  BN10 39 B2
Temple Gdns BN1 16 B3
Temple St BN1 16 B3
Tennis Cl BN27 25 D5
Tennis Rd BN3 30 A1
Tennyson Walk BN23 40 A6
Tenterden Rise TN34 26 A2
Terminus Av TN39 14 B4
Terminus Pl,
  Brighton BN1 17 E1
Terminus Pl,
  Hailsham BN27 25 D6
Terminus Rd,
  Bexhill TN39 14 B4
Terminus Rd,
  Brighton BN1 17 E1
Terminus Rd,
  Eastbourne BN21 21 F3
Terminus St BN1 17 E1
Terrace Rd TN37 50 C4
Testers Cotts TN35 56 C2
Thakenham Cl TN40 15 G2
Thames Cl BN2 17 H2
Thanet Way TN34 26 A2
The Acorns BN27 25 D5
The Albermarle BN2 16 C4
The Avenue,
  Eastbourne BN21 21 E3
The Avenue,
  Hailsham BN27 25 D6
The Avenue,
  Hastings TN35 26 D2
The Avenue,
  Heathfield TN21 28 C2
The Avenue,
  Lewes BN7 32 D5
The Avenue,
  Mayfield TN20 23 B1
The Beechings BN24 41 G3
The Belfry BN27 25 D5
The Bernhard Baron
  Cottage Homes BN26 42 C2
The Boulevard BN24 41 G3
The Boundary BN25 49 E5
The Bourne TN34 26 C5
The Briary TN40 15 F5
The Bricky BN10 39 B2
The Broadway,
  Hastings TN35 26 D2
The Broadway,
  Polegate BN26 42 C2
The Broyle BN8 47 B4
The Byeway TN34 26 A2
The Byeways BN25 49 E5
The Byeways BN25 49 E5
The Causeway BN25 48 B3
The Cedars BN27 25 D5
The Chantry BN21 21 E3
The Chartres TN40 15 F5
The Cheviots TN34 26 A2

TN32 51 C5
, 13 C1
s TN37 50 D4
ugh TN6 18 C3
N35 23 A4
BN9 36 F3
ye TN31 46 B2
N25 49 F6
s BN21 21 E1
, 13 F4
TN34 26 A4
BN7 33 E5
ard TN34 26 A4
BN25 49 E6
nt,
e RN20 42 C6
nt,
BN9 36 F3
N34 26 C5
way BN41 43 A1
TN31 46 C3
ne BN20 42 C6
Uckfield TN22 52 E3
ns BN20 20 D5
ks BN27 25 C6
ough TN6 18 B4
BN27 25 D7
Hove BN3 30 D5
ld TN22 34 A2
en BN9 37 C8
rds TN38 50 A3
Uckfield TN22 52 C4
orsebridge
24 E1
BN9 37 E5
eway BN3 30 C2
ocks BN6 35 B5
BN8 47 A3
made BN10 45 H6
ay,
N39 14 A2
ay,
ven BN9 37 A6
ings TN6 19 E3
es TN40 15 F4
ngs BN26 12 B2
es TN34 26 A1
es BN27 25 F6
ps BN7 32 D4
dens BN41 43 B3
e,
am BN27 25 B8
e,
ld TN20 23 B1
de,
d TN22 53 D5
des TN40 15 E3
be TN34 26 C3
belands TN6 18 D4
n TN22 52 D3
ffs BN21 20 D2
een,
ton BN2 44 B3
een,
borough TN6 18 D4
een,
am BN27 24 D3
een, Hove BN3 38 D1
, Lewes BN8 38 D1
, Rye TN31 46 C4
n,
ards TN38 50 B2
n Walk BN22 42 D6
ys BN20 20 C2
ve, Battle TN33 13 F4
ve,
borough TN6 18 C5
ve,
ourne BN20 42 C6
ve,
am BN27 25 D8
ove,
ield TN20 23 B1
ove,
haven BN9 36 E3
ove, Rye TN31 46 C2
en BN27 25 E7
awthorns BN27 25 C6

The Heights TN35 27 G1
The Highlands TN39 14 A1
The Highway,
Newhaven BN9 37 A7
The Highway,
Peacehaven BN10 39 E3
The Hollies TN20 23 B1
The Hollow,
Newhaven BN9 36 D2
The Hollow, Rye TN31 38 B5
The Holt,
Hailsham BN27 25 C4
The Holt, Seaford BN25 49 E2
The Jackdaws TN22 53 E7
The Jays TN22 53 E7
The Lanes BN1 17 E5
The Laurels TN22 52 E4
The Lawn TN38 50 C4
The Lawns BN27 25 E7
The Leas,
Peacehaven BN10 39 E4
The Leas, Wadhurst TN5 54 F1
The Limes BN21 20 D1
The Link TN31 46 A3
The Links TN38 50 A3
The Linkway BN24 40 A3
The Lords BN25 49 E1
The Lowlands BN27 24 C4
The Lynchets BN7 33 G2
The Manse TN20 23 B1
The Marplit TN5 54 D2
The Martlets,
Crowborough TN6 18 D5
The Martlets,
Hailsham BN27 25 C6
The Martlets,
Lewes BN7 33 G2
The Martletts BN8 47 B3
The Meadows,
Crowborough TN6 18 D4
The Meadows,
Lewes BN7 33 G2
The Mews BN8 49 G3
The Mill Race BN20 42 C5
The Mint TN31 46 C3
The Moorings BN20 20 D5
The Mount,
Hailsham BN27 25 D7
The Mount,
St Leonards TN38 50 B4
The Mount,
Uckfield TN22 52 C4
The Nightingales TN22 53 E7
The Nook TN22 53 E7
The Oakfield TN31 46 C1
The Oaks TN21 28 D3
The Paddock, Hove BN3 30 D2
The Paddock, Rye TN31 38 B6
The Paddock,
Uckfield TN22 3? A3
The Paddocks BN27 24 C3
The Parade, Hove BN3 43 D1
The Parade,
Pevensey BN24 41 F4
The Parade,
The Square, Pevensey
BN24 41 G3
The Paragon BN20 42 B6
The Park, Brighton BN2 44 C4
The Park,
Crowborough TN6 18 D4
The Peverells BN25 49 F2
The Plat TN31 38 B6
The Potteries TN22 53 E8
The Promenade,
Peacehaven BN10 39 B3
The Promenade,
Peacehaven BN10 45 H6
The Quadrant RN21 20 D1
The Quay TN31 46 B3
The Quentins BN27 25 D6
The Ridge,
Hastings TN35 27 E1
The Ridge,
Winchelsea TN36 55 D5
The Ridgeway,
Hailsham BN27 29 A1
The Ridgeway,
Seaford BN25 49 E3
The Ridings,
Bexhill TN39 14 A1
The Ridings,
Lewes BN8 38 B2
The Ridings,
Seaford BN25 49 E2
The Rise TN21 29 A5
The Rising BN23 40 A6
The Rose Walk BN9 37 B6
The Rotyngs BN2 44 B3
The Rough BN8 38 C2
The Sanctuary BN20 20 A1
The Shepway BN25 49 H3

The Smithy TN22 53 C6
The Spinney,
Battle TN33 13 F4
The Spinney,
Hastings TN34 26 A4
The Spinney,
Heathfield TN21 28 D3
The Spinney,
Robertsbridge TN32 51 B6
The Spinneys BN7 33 G3
The Square,
Hailsham BN27 25 C7
The Square,
Pevensey BN24 41 G3
The Square,
Wadhurst TN5 54 F3
The Steyne BN25 49 E5
The Stiles BN27 25 E6
The Stringwalk BN27 25 E7
The Suttons TN31 34 C6
The Thatchings BN26 42 C4
The Triangle BN20 42 D6
The Twitten,
Brighton BN2 44 B4
The Twitten,
Crowborough TN6 18 C5
The Twitten,
Pevensey BN24 41 E4
The Tye BN26 12 C3
The Uplands TN38 50 B4
The Upper Dr BN3 30 D3
The Village Meads
BN20 20 D5
The Warren,
Mayfield TN20 23 D1
The Warren,
Wadhurst TN5 51 C2
Theaklen Dr TN38 50 B1
Theobalds Grn TN21 28 C4
Third Av, Bexhill TN40 15 G3
Third Av, Hove BN3 30 C6
Third Av,
Newhaven BN9 37 C6
Third Rd BN10 39 A2
Thomas Cl BN26 42 C3
Thomas St BN7 33 G3
Thompson Rd BN9 36 E3
Thornbank Cres TN39 14 A5
Thorny TN21 28 C2
Three Oaks La TN5 54 B1
Thurrock Cl BN20 42 D5
Thwaites La TN31 38 B5
Ticehurst Cl TN34 26 D1
Tichborne St BN1 17 E3
Tideswell Rd BN21 21 F2
Tidy St BN1 17 F2
Tilbury Pl BN2 17 G3
Tilbury Way BN2 17 H3
Tilehurst Dr BN27 25 C5
Tilekiln La TN38 27 G1
Tillingham Av TN31 46 B3
Tillington Ter*,
Ashburnham Rd TN34 26 D3
Tillstone St BN2 17 H4
Tilsmore Rd TN21 28 B2
Timber Yard Cotts BN7 33 G4
Timber Yard La BN7 33 G4
Timberdown TN21 28 C1
Timberlaine Rd BN24 40 D5
Timberley Gdns TN22 53 E8
Timbers BN27 25 E6
Timberyard La BN7 32 C2
Tinkers La TN5 51 C1
Tisbury Rd BN3 30 D5
Tithe Barn Fld TN36 31 C2
Titian Rd BN3 30 A4
Tiverton Dr TN40 15 F4
Toll Wood Rd TN21 29 B6
Tollgates TN33 13 A3
Tollwood Pk TN6 19 F5
Tollwood Rd TN6 19 F5
Tompsets Bank RH18 22 C4
Tomtits La RH18 22 B4
Tonbridge Way TN31 34 B5
Tongdean Av BN3 30 D1
Top Cross Rd TN40 15 G2
Torfield Cl TN34 26 D4
Torfield Rd BN21 21 E1
Toronto Ter,
Brighton BN2 17 H2
Toronto Ter, Lewes BN7 32 A1
Torrance Cl BN3 30 A3
Tott Yew Rd BN20 42 C5
Tower Cl BN24 41 G2
Tower Mill Pl BN26 42 C4
Tower Rd BN7 50 C2
Tower Rd West TN38 50 B3
Tower Ride TN22 52 E3
Tower St,
Heathfield TN21 28 D1
Tower St, Rye TN31 46 C3
Tower Vw TN22 52 D4
Town Hall Sq TN39 14 C5
Townlands Rd TN5 54 E3

Trafalgar Ct BN1 17 F1
Trafalgar La BN1 17 E2
Trafalgar Pl BN1 17 E1
Trafalgar Rd BN41 43 A3
Trafalgar St BN1 17 E1
Trafalgar Street Arches
BN1 17 E1
Trafalgar Ter BN1 17 E2
Transit Rd BN9 37 D6
Travellers La TN35 27 E1
Treblers Rd TN6 19 H6
Tredcroft Rd BN3 30 D1
Tremola Av BN2 44 D3
Trenches Rd TN6 18 D5
Trinity Fld BN8 47 B2
Trinity Pl BN21 21 F3
Trinity St*,
Robertson St TN34 26 A5
Trinity Trees BN21 21 F3
Trinity Villas*,
White Rock Rd TN34 26 A6
Troon Cl BN25 48 A1
Troy Cl TN6 19 E5
Tubwell La TN6 19 H6
Tudor Av TN38 50 A4
Tudor Cl, Brighton BN2 44 C3
Tudor Cl, Hove BN3 30 A2
Tudor Cl, Seaford BN25 48 C3
Tudor Ct TN39 14 A5
Tumulus Rd BN2 44 D2
Tunbridge Wells Rd
TN20 23 C1
Tuppenney Cl TN34 26 D1
Turkey Rd TN39 14 A1
Turkeycock La*,
Conduit Hill TN31 46 C3
Turnberry Dr BN27 25 B6
Turner Cl TN40 15 E3
Turners Green La TN5 54 E1
Turners Green Rd TN5 54 E1
Turnpike Cl BN8 47 D1
Tuscan Ct BN10 45 H6
Twyfords TN6 18 C5
Tye Cl BN2 45 F5
Tye Vw BN10 45 H4
Tyedean Rd BN10 45 G5
Tyhurst Pl TN22 53 D6
Tyson Pl BN2 17 H4

Uckfield By-Pass TN22 52 A4
Uckham La TN33 13 D1
Udimore Rd TN31 46 A4
Undercliff TN38 50 B5
Underhill TN22 34 B3
Union Cl BN27 24 D3
Union Point TN22 53 D7
Union St, Brighton BN1 17 E4
Union St,
St Leonards TN38 50 C4
Upland Rd BN20 20 B3
Uplands Cl,
Bexhill TN39 14 A2
Uplands Cl,
Uckfield TN22 52 D3
Upper Av BN21 21 F1
Upper Belgrave Rd
BN25 49 E3
Upper Broomgrove Rd
TN34 26 C2
Upper Carlisle Rd BN20 20 B5
Upper Chyngton Gdns
BN25 49 G3
Upper Cl RH18 22 C3
Upper Clarence Rd
TN37 50 C1
Upper Dukes Dr BN20 20 C6
Upper Gardner St BN1 17 E3
Upper Gloucester Rd
BN1 16 D2
Upper Horsebridge Rd
BN27 24 C3
Upper Lake TN33 13 D3
Upper Market St BN3 16 A3
Upper Maze Hill TN38 50 B3
Upper North St BN1 16 C3
Upper Park Rd BN2 17 H4
Upper Park Rd TN37 50 C2
Upper Platts TN5 51 D2
Upper Rock Gdns BN2 17 H5
Upper St James's St
BN2 17 H5
Upper Sea Rd TN40 14 D5
Upper Sherwood Rd
BN25 49 F3
Upper South Rd TN37 50 C2
Upper Sq RH18 22 C2
Upper Station Rd TN21 28 D2
Upper Valley Rd BN9 37 A6
Upperton Gdns BN21 21 E2
Upperton La BN21 21 E2
Upperton Rd BN21 20 D1
Upwick Rd BN20 20 B2

Val Prinseps Rd BN24 41 E5

Vale Cl BN25 49 G3
Vale Gdns BN41 43 B4
Vale Rd, Battle TN33 13 A3
Vale Rd, Mayfield TN20 23 C2
Vale Rd, Portslade-by-Sea
BN41 43 B4
Vale Rd,
St Leonards TN37 50 C1
Vale Rd, Saltdean BN2 45 E2
Vale Rd, Seaford BN25 49 E4
Vale View Rd TN21 28 C3
Valence Rd BN7 32 D4
Valerie Cl BN41 43 B1
Vallance Gdns BN3 30 B6
Vallance Rd BN3 30 B5
Vallensdean Cotts BN41 43 B1
Valley Cl, Brighton BN41 43 A1
Valley Cl,
Newhaven BN9 37 B5
Valley Dene BN9 37 B6
Valley Dr BN25 49 F3
Valley Rd,
Crowborough TN6 18 D5
Valley Rd, Lewes BN7 32 D5
Valley Rd,
Newhaven BN9 37 A6
Valley Rise BN25 49 E3
Valley View Cl TN6 18 D5
Valleyside BN734 26 D2
Vantage Walk TN38 50 B1
Vega Cl BN25 25 F6
Ventnor Villas BN3 30 C5
Venture Cl TN40 15 F4
Vernon Av BN10 39 D3
Vernon Cl TN22 53 D6
Vernon Gdns BN1 16 C1
Vernon Rd TN22 53 D6
Vernon Ter BN1 16 C1
Vernons Rd BN8 38 C2
Veronica Way BN2 17 H5
Verralls Walk BN7 33 E6
Vicarage Cl, Lewes BN8 47 A3
Vicarage Cl,
Seaford BN25 49 E4
Vicarage Dr BN20 20 C2
Vicarage Fld BN27 25 E6
Vicarage La,
Brighton BN2 44 B3
Vicarage La,
Eastbourne BN20 20 C2
Vicarage La,
Hailsham BN27 25 D5
Vicarage La,
Hastings TN35 56 B2
Vicarage Rd,
Eastbourne BN20 20 C2
Vicarage Rd,
Hailsham BN27 25 E6
Vicarage Rd,
Hastings TN34 26 C4
Vicarage Ter BN2 44 B4
Vicarage Way BN8 47 A3
Vicarge Cl BN9 36 E3
Victor Cl BN25 48 D3
Victoria Av,
Hastings TN35 27 E1
Victoria Av,
Peacehaven BN10 39 C3
Victoria Cl,
Polegate BN26 42 C2
Victoria Cl,
Uckfield TN22 52 D4
Victoria Ct TN38 50 B5
Victoria Dr BN20 20 B1
Victoria Gdns BN20 20 B1
Victoria Gro BN3 30 D5
Victoria Mews*,
West St BN3 44 B4
Victoria Pl BN1 16 C2
Victoria Rd,
Bexhill TN39 14 C5
Victoria Rd,
Brighton BN1 16 B2
Victoria Rd,
Crowborough TN6 19 G6
Victoria Rd,
Eastbourne BN20 20 B1
Victoria Rd,
Hailsham BN27 25 D6
Victoria Rd,
Herstmonceux BN27 29 C2
Victoria Rd,
Mayfield TN20 23 A1
Victoria Rd,
Polegate BN26 42 C2
Victoria Rd, Portslade-by-Sea
BN41 43 A3
Victoria Rd,
St Leonards TN37 50 D4
Victoria St BN1 16 C3
Victoria Ter BN3 30 C6
Victoria Way TN36 55 C5
View Bank TN35 27 F2
View Rd BN10 39 C3

Views Wood Path TN22 52 E3
Viking Cl BN25 48 A1
Villa Rd TN37 50 D4
Vine Pl BN1 16 C2
Vine St BN1 17 F3
Vines Cross Rd TN21 29 B5
Vineyard La TN5 51 A1
Virgins Cft TN33 13 C1
Virgins La TN33 13 C1

Wadhurst Par TN5 54 E3
Wainwright Rd TN39 14 C5
Waite Cl BN7 33 G3
Waites La TN35 23 D2
Waldegrave St TN34 26 B4
Waldene Cl TN34 26 B2
Waldon Ter TN33 13 D3
Waldron Ct TN21 28 C1
Waldron Thorns TN21 28 B3
Waldshut BN7 32 D2
Walesbeech Rd BN2 45 E5
Wall Hill Rd RH18 22 B1
Wallands Cres BN7 33 F4
Wallis Cl TN6 19 E5
Wallsend Rd BN2 40 D3
Walmer Rd TN38 49 H4
Walnut Cl TN21 28 D3
Walnut Walk BN26 42 C3
Walsingham Rd BN3 30 A5
Walton Pk TN39 14 A5
Walwers La BN7 32 B2
Wanderdown Cl BN2 44 A1
Wanderdown Dr BN2 44 A1
Wanderdown Rd BN2 44 A1
Wanderdown Way BN2 44 A1
Wannock Av BN2 42 B5
Wannock Cl TN40 15 G3
Wannock Dr BN26 42 C4
Wannock Gdns BN26 42 B6
Wannock La BN20 42 B5
Wannock Rd BN26 42 B5
Warburton Cl TN22 52 D4
Ward Cl TN5 54 D3
Ward Way TN39 14 A3
Wardsbrook Rd TN5 51 B3
Wares Fld TN22 53 E8
Wares Rd TN22 53 E8
Warminster Rd BN24 41 E4
Warren Cl,
  Crowborough TN6 18 C4
Warren Cl,
  Eastbourne BN20 20 B5
Warren Cl, Lewes BN7 32 D5
Warren Cotts TN30 23 D1
Warren Dr BN7 32 D5
Warren Gate TN6 18 C4
Warren Hill BN20 20 A4
Warren Rd,
  Crowborough TN6 18 A5
Warren Rd,
  Hastings TN35 23 A4
Warren Ridge TN6 18 B4
Warren Way BN10 45 H4
Warrior Cl BN41 43 B1
Warriors Gdns TN37 50 C4
Warrior Sq,
  Eastbourne BN22 21 G1
Warrior Sq,
  St Leonards TN37 50 C4
Warwick Cl BN27 24 E3
Warwick Rd,
  Bexhill TN39 14 A4
Warwick Rd,
  Seaford BN25 49 E4
Washington St BN2 17 H1
Washwell La TN5 54 E4
Watchbell La TN31 46 C3
Watchbell St TN31 46 C4
Watergate TN39 14 C1
Watergate La BN7 32 A2
Waterloo Pl,
  Brighton BN2 17 G1
Waterloo Pl, Lewes BN7 32 B1
Waterloo Pl*,
  The Bourne TN34 26 D5
Waterloo Sq BN26 12 B2
Waterloo St BN3 16 A4
Watermens Cl TN34 26 A2
Watermill Cl,
  Bexhill TN39 14 C1
Watermill Cl,
  Polegate BN26 42 C4
Watermill La,
  Bexhill TN39 14 C1
Watermill La,
  Hastings TN35,36 31 A3

Waters Cotts TN5 54 F4
Waterside Cl TN34 26 D2
Waterworks Rd,
  Eastbourne BN22 21 F1
Waterworks Rd,
  Hastings TN34 26 B4
Wattles Wish TN33 13 C1
Watts Cl TN5 54 E3
Watts La BN21 20 D1
Waverley Gdns BN24 41 E4
Wayfield Av BN3 30 A2
Wayfield Cl BN3 30 A2
Wayside Walk TN21 28 B3
Weald Av BN9 37 A7
Weald Cl BN7 33 E4
Weald Vw TN5 54 F1
Wealden Cl TN6 18 D3
Wealdview Rd TN21 28 A2
Weavers La BN26 12 C2
Weaversbrook La TN21 28 E4
Week La BN8 47 B6
Welbeck Av, Hove BN3 43 D5
Welbeck Av,
  St Leonards TN38 50 A5
Welesmere Rd BN2 44 C2
Wellcombe Cres BN20 20 C6
Wellesley Cl TN6 18 B5
Wellesley Ct TN34 26 C5
Wellesley Rd BN21 21 F2
Wellhouse Pl BN7 33 E5
Wellington Cl TN6 13 C2
Wellington Mews TN34 26 B4
Wellington Pk BN25 49 F4
Wellington Pl TN34 26 B5
Wellington Rd,
  Brighton BN41 43 A5
Wellington Rd,
  Hastings TN34 26 B5
Wellington Rd,
  Newhaven BN9 36 E3
Wellington Rd,
  Peacehaven BN10 39 E3
Wellington Sq TN34 26 B5
Wellington St BN7 32 B1
Wellis Gdns TN38 50 A3
Wellplace Cotts TN36 31 D2
Wells Cl BN20 20 B5
Went Hill Gdns BN22 42 D6
Went Hill Pk BN25 49 F4
Wentworth Cl,
  Bexhill TN40 15 G3
Wentworth Cl,
  Hailsham BN27 24 B4
Wentworth St BN2 17 G5
Wesley Mews TN5 54 C4
West Ascent TN38 50 B5
West Beeches Rd TN6 19 E4
West Cl, Alfriston BN26 12 B2
West Cl, Polegate BN26 42 D2
West Dean Rise BN25 49 F3
West Down Rd TN39 14 B4
West Dr BN2 17 H4
West End BN27 29 A1
West Hill Pl BN1 16 D1
West Hill Rd,
  Brighton BN1 16 C1
West Hill Rd,
  St Leonards TN38 50 A5
West Hill St BN1 16 D1
West Par TN39 14 B6
West Point BN8 38 B2
West Quay BN9 37 D6
West Rd BN41 43 A4
West St, Brighton BN1 16 D5
West St,
  Eastbourne BN21 21 E3
West St, Hassocks BN6 35 B5
West St, Hastings TN34 26 C5
West St, Lewes BN7 32 A1
West St, Mayfield TN20 23 A3
West St, Polegate BN26 12 B1
West St, Portslade-by-Sea
  BN41 43 B5
West St,
  Rottingdean BN2 44 B4
West St, Rye TN31 46 C3
West St, Seaford BN25 48 D5
West Ter,
  Eastbourne BN21 21 E3
West Ter,
  Hailsham BN27 29 A1
West Undercliff TN31 46 A5
West View Ct BN25 48 D5
West Vw, Hastings TN34 26 D3
West Vw, Hove BN3 30 D4
West Vw, Seaford BN25 48 D5

West Vw, Uckfield TN22 52 D3
West Way,
  Crowborough TN6 18 C1
West Way, Hove BN3 43 C1
Westaway Dr TN39 14 B5
Westbourne Gdns BN3 30 B5
Westbourne Gro BN3 30 B4
Westbourne Pl BN3 30 B5
Westbourne St BN3 30 B5
Westbourne Villas BN3 30 B6
Westbrook BN2 44 A2
Westbrook La TN35 56 C1
Westcourt Dr TN39 14 A5
Westdean Av BN9 37 A7
Westdown Rd BN25 48 D4
Westerleigh Cl TN38 50 A3
Western Av, Battle TN33 13 C3
Western Av,
  Polegate BN26 42 D2
Western Esp BN41 43 C5
Western Gdns TN6 19 G6
Western Par BN20 21 E6
Western Rd,
  Bexhill TN40 14 C5
Western Rd,
  Brighton BN1,3 16 A3
Western Rd,
  Crowborough TN6 19 G6
Western Rd,
  Eastbourne BN22 21 G1
Western Rd,
  Hailsham BN27 25 B6
Western Rd, Lewes BN7 33 E4
Western Rd,
  Newhaven BN9 37 B6
Western Rd,
  Newick BN8 38 B2
Western Rd,
  Pevensey BN24 41 E5
Western Rd,
  St Leonards TN37 50 C4
Western Rd,
  Wadhurst TN5 54 E2
Western St BN1 16 A4
Western Ter BN1 16 B3
Westfield Av BN2 45 E2
Westfield Av North BN2 45 F2
Westfield Av South BN2 45 F2
Westfield Cl BN26 42 D2
Westfield Ct BN26 42 D2
Westfield La TN35 56 C3
Westfield Rise BN2 45 F2
Westgate St BN7 32 A2
Westham By-Pass BN24 40 A2
Westham Dr BN24 41 G3
Westmeston Av BN2 44 D5
Westminster Cres TN34 26 C1
Westview Ter BN9 36 D3
Westville Rd TN39 14 B5
Wharf Rd,
  Eastbourne BN21 21 F2
Wharf Rd, Hove BN3 43 D5
Whatlington Rd TN33 13 D1
Wheatsheaf Gdns BN7 33 H3
Wheel La TN35 56 A1
Whiffens Cl BN27 25 C7
Whincroft Pk TN6 18 B6
Whipping Post La BN2 44 B3
White Ct BN26 12 B3
White Hill BN7 32 A1
White Rock TN37 26 A6
White Rock Gdns TN34 26 A6
White Rock Rd TN37 26 A6
White St BN2 17 G4
White Way BN26 12 B3
Whitebread La TN31 38 D4
Whitecross St BN1 17 F1
Whitefriars Rd TN34 26 C4
Whitehill Cl TN6 18 D5
Whitehill Rd TN6 18 D5
Whitehouse Av TN39 14 R2
Whiteway BN25 49 E1
Whiteway La BN2 44 B3
Whitley Rd BN22 21 F1
Whittingtons Way TN34 26 C1
Wick Hall BN3 16 A2
Wickham Av TN39 14 B6
Wickham Rock Rd TN36 55 A4
Wicklands Av BN2 45 E4
Wilbury Av BN3 30 D3
Wilbury Gdns BN3 30 D3
Wilbury Gro BN3 30 D5
Wilbury Rd BN3 30 D5
Wilbury Villas BN3 30 D4
Wilderness Gdns TN31 38 B5
Wilderness Pk TN6 18 C4

Wilfred Rd BN3 43 D3
Wilkins Way TN40 15 G2
Wilkinson Cl BN2 44 B2
Wilkinson Way BN25 49 E3
William St,
  Brighton BN2 17 G4
William St, Portslade-by-Sea
  BN41 43 A4
Willingdon Av TN39 14 B4
Willingdon Ct BN20 42 D6
Willingdon Rd BN21 20 C1
Willow Av BN27 24 D4
Willow Bank TN32 51 C6
Willow Cl TN21 28 D1
Willow Dr,
  Polegate BN26 42 C4
Willow Dr,
  Seaford BN25 49 H4
Willow End TN34 26 B1
Willow La TN36 55 D4
Willow Mews TN32 51 C6
Willow Walk BN9 37 B5
Willowdowne Cl BN26 42 C4
Willowfield Cr BN22 21 G2
Willowfield Sq BN22 21 G2
Willowmead TN6 18 C6
Wilmington Gdns BN21 21 F4
Wilmington Rd,
  Hastings TN34 26 C2
Wilmington Rd,
  Newhaven BN9 37 A7
Wilmington Rd,
  Seaford BN25 48 D4
Wilmington Sq BN21 21 F4
Wilson Gro TN22 53 B5
Wilton Rd TN40 14 D6
Winchcombe Rd BN22 21 F1
Winchelsea Cl BN25 49 H3
Winchelsea Rd,
  Hastings TN35 27 E1
Winchelsea Rd,
  Rye TN31 46 B4
Windgrove Cotts TN33 13 D1
Windgrove Ho TN33 13 D1
Winding St*,
  The Bourne TN34 26 C5
Windlesham Av BN1 16 B1
Windlesham Cl BN41 43 A2
Windlesham Gdns BN1 16 B1
Windlesham Rd BN1 16 B2
Windmill Cl,
  Heathfield TN21 28 D1
Windmill Cl, Hove BN3 30 A1
Windmill Cl,
  Pevensey BN24 40 B3
Windmill Ct TN36 55 C3
Windmill Dr TN39 14 B2
Windmill Hill BN27 29 C2
Windmill La TN5 54 C3
Windmill Pl BN26 42 C4
Windmill Rd,
  Polegate BN26 42 D4
Windmill Rd,
  St Leonards TN38 50 B1
Windmill St BN2 17 H3
Windmill Ter BN2 17 H2
Windmill Way TN36 55 D3
Windover Cres BN7 32 D3
Windover Way BN22 42 D5
Windsor Cl BN25 48 A1
Windsor Pl TN6 19 G6
Windsor Rd,
  Bexhill TN39 14 C5
Windsor Rd,
  Crowborough TN6 19 G6
Windsor Rd,
  Hailsham BN27 25 D7
Windsor St BN1 17 E4
Windsor Way,
  Polegate BN26 42 C2
Windsor Way,
  Winchelsea TN36 55 C5
Wineham Way TN40 15 F4
Wingate Cl TN38 50 A2
Winscot Cl TN6 18 C5
Winston Dr TN39 14 A5
Winterbourne Cl,
  Hastings TN34 50 D3
Winterbourne Cl,
  Lewes BN7 32 D6
Winterbourne Hollow
  BN7 32 D5
Winterbourne La BN7 32 D5
Winterbourne Mews
  BN7 33 E5
Winton Av BN2 45 E2

Winton St BN26
Wish Rd,
  Brighton BN41
Wish Rd,
  Eastbourne BN2...
Wish St TN31
Wish Ward TN31
Withyham Av BN2
Wivelsfield Rd BN2
Woburn Cl BN27
Wolfe Cl TN6
Wolseley Rd BN41
Wood Cl BN2
Woodbine La BN8
Woodbrook Rd TN2...
Woodcombe TN34
Woodcote Rd RH18
Woodhams Cl TN33...
Woodhouse Cl BN3
Woodhouse Rd BN3...
Woodland Av BN3
Woodland Cl BN3
Woodland Dr BN3
Woodland Mews TN...
Woodland Rise TN40...
Woodland Vale Rd T...
Woodland Way,
  Crowborough TN6
Woodland Way,
  Hastings TN35
Woodland Way,
  Heathfield TN21
Woodlands,
  Crowborough TN6
Woodlands, Hove BN...
Woodlands Cl,
  Hailsham BN27
Woodlands Cl,
  Heathfield TN21
Woodlands Cl,
  Uckfield TN22
Woodpecker Dr BN2...
Woodpecker Way TN...
Woodroffe Lodge TN...
Woodruff Av BN3
Woods Pass*,
  All Saints St TN34
Woodsgate Av TN40
Woodsgate Pk TN39
Woodside TN6
Woodville Rd TN39
Worcester Villas BN3
Worcester Way BN27
Wordsworth St BN3
Workhouse La,
  Hastings TN35
Workhouse La,
  Winchelsea TN36
Worsham La TN40
Wren Cl TN21
Wren Cl TN33
Wrestwood Cl TN40
Wrestwood Rd TN40
Wychurst Gdns TN40
Wykeham Rd TN34
Wykenham Ter BN1
Wyndham St BN2
Wynne Mews BN3

Yarrow Rd BN7
Yates Cl TN31
Yeomans BN8
Yew Tree Cl,
  Heathfield TN21
Yew Tree Cl, Lewes BN8
York Av BN3
York Gdns TN34
York Pl BN1
York Rd, Bexhill TN40
York Rd,
  Eastbourne BN21
York Rd, Hove BN3
York Rd,
  Peacehaven BN10
York Rd,
  St Leonards TN37
Youl Grange BN20

Zion Gdns BN1